VANISHING MARKERS

Memories of Boston and Maine Railroading, 1946-1952

RALPH E. FISHER

THE STEPHEN GREENE PRESS

Brattleboro, Vermont ✧ **Publishers of the Shortline RR Series**

ACKNOWLEDGMENTS

with grateful thanks to—

    DONALD S. ROBINSON

    THE EDAVILLE MUSEUM OF NEW ENGLAND HERITAGE

    EDGAR T. MEAD

    NEW ENGLAND RAIL SERVICE

    PHILIP R. HASTINGS

    THE 470 RAILROAD CLUB, PORTLAND DIVISION, RRE

    THE RAILWAY AND LOCOMOTIVE HISTORICAL SOCIETY

    HERMAN SHANER

—for assistance in gathering
and permission to use the photographs
appearing in this book, as credited
on pages vi and vii following.

COPYRIGHT

This book has been produced in the United States of America:
designed by R. Dike Hamilton, composed by Publishers Composition Service,
printed and bound by Halliday Lithograph Corp.
It is published by The Stephen Greene Press, Brattleboro, Vermont 05301

Library of Congress Cataloging in Publication Data
Fisher, Ralph E. 1920–
    Vanishing markers.

    (A Shortline RR series special)
    1. Fisher, Ralph E., 1920– 2. Boston and
Maine Railroad. I. Title.
TF140.F54A37   385′.0974   76-15577
ISBN 0-8289-0287-9

76 77 78 79 80 81 9 8 7 6 5 4 3 2 1

How things were on the old B&M

FOREWORD

HERE, IN THE UNVARNISHED PLAIN TALK OF A REAL RAILROADER, IS THE STORY OF how things were on the old Boston & Maine. You sweat with author Ralph Fisher on a Boston to Portland steam-hauled freight during a humid summer night, and then you're with him freezing to death on a wintry snow-plow extra up the main line. He gives you all the no-frills anxiety and frustration of railroading combined with its own particular rewards.

It is hard to imagine, in the Bicentennial year 1976, how much railroading has changed since the late 1940s–early '50s period in which the action of this story takes place. Those were the years of transition from steam to diesel locomotives and the phasing out of passenger service. Yet, as a finalizing verdict, virtually none of B&M's steam-bumping diesels have lasted into the Bicentennial.

Eventually there will be a full history of the Boston & Maine Railroad, and it will be a long yarn to tell. It will remain for some future veteran of the road to recount the experiences and anecdotes associated with unit trains, Turboliners, containerization, welded rail, concrete ties and other innovations coming as an answer to the energy crisis and the desire in this country to do things better.

Meanwhile, Ralph Fisher, now serving as curator of the Museum of New England Heritage at the Edaville RR in South Carver, Massachusetts, has written *Vanishing Markers* to trigger memories of old-style railroading in every reader's imagination—as it did in mine. There's the caboose about to trundle by! Better jump on board, draw up to the stove, and enjoy a veteran railroader's tale. . . .

EDGAR T. MEAD
Author. Elected Official. Transportation Economist

CONTENTS

PHOTOS AND CREDITS

TITLE PAGE. Boston engine terminal, East Somerville, Mass., in 1950. Pacifics, Moguls, switchers waiting for assignments during the midday. Photo by EDGAR T. MEAD

PAGE V. B&M Pacific 3648 highballs north of Boston shortly before dieselization with a train of secondhand steel coaches, including a head-end "Wyatt Earp" open end combination car obtained from the Delaware, Lackawanna & Western RR. Courtesy of THE RAILWAY & LOCOMOTIVE HISTORICAL SOCIETY

PAGE 9. Engine No. 3715, a Class P-4b Pacific built by Lima in 1937, is shown here in the North Station during September of that year about to steam off with the *Kennebec Limited* at 9:40 A.M., destination Bangor, Me. Later dubbed *Kwasind* in B&M's engine-naming program, 3715 pulled the first train the author worked on, No. 332, Concord to Boston. R. P. Morris photo from the EDAVILLE MUSEUM collection

PAGE 11. Mogul No. 1455 gets some tender loving care from her engineer prior to hauling train No. 3106 out of Clinton, Mass. DONALD S. ROBINSON photo

PAGE 12. EDGAR T. MEAD captured this ruminative moment between engine men on B&M premises at Middlesex Yard, Lowell.

PAGE 17. Engine 2648 on train 4308 ambles into the diamond at Waumbek Jct., N.H. Photo by DONALD S. ROBINSON

PAGE 21. Hale St. bridge, supporting old signal installation at Lowell, Mass., casts late afternoon shadow on tracks and rods below, as train No. 309, powered by Pacific 3679, sits in the sun. DONALD S. ROBINSON photo

PAGE 23, *top.* Early morning commuter train about to depart from Bedford, Mass., in "accommodation train" days. Engine No. 3662 is on the point. *Bottom:* A Color Light three-arm pole looks down on steam and diesel power confrontation, as train Nos. 54 and B-9 meet at Ayer, Mass., May 19, 1947. Both photos, DONALD S. ROBINSON

PAGE 25. Extra 1450 jogs into Nashua, N.H., from Hillsboro. Photo by DONALD S. ROBINSON

PAGE 27. Water facility in Middlesex Yard, Lowell. Photo by EDGAR T. MEAD

PAGE 28, *top.* EDAVILLE MUSEUM. *Center:* NEW ENGLAND RAIL SERVICE. *Bottom:* EDAVILLE MUSEUM

PAGE 31. Displaying the white flags of an extra, 2–8–0 No. 2413 sits idle for a moment at Middlesex Yard. EDGAR T. MEAD photo

PAGE 33. Engine 3000, a 2–10–2 Santa Fe type, built Schenectady 1920. Sold to Maine Central 1937. Scrapped 1951. Similar engines were renumbered in the 2900's. Photo from EDAVILLE MUSEUM collection

PAGE 34. Tank of Mogul 1493 in a difficulty similar to that of the switch-splitting "mudsucker" described in the accompanying text. Location unknown, the photo is from the EDAVILLE MUSEUM collection

PAGE 36. The train is MP-2 and pusher 2–8–0 No. 2714 is "stack talking" to the rear platform of one of B&M's "newer steel buggies" on the Connecticut River bridge just east of East Deerfield yard. Photo by DONALD S. ROBINSON

PAGES 38–39. No. 4226 EMD F2A and FTB

units ignore a trackside water plug in Somerville yards, Boston. Photo, from EDAVILLE MUSEUM, dates back to March 11, 1947.

PAGE 40. June, 1949. Hind end of through freight JD-1, dispatched out of White River Jct., is passing slowly across 800 feet of B&M trestle over Androscoggin River and the Grand Trunk Montreal-Portland main line near Gorham, N.H. Headed by diesels Nos. 4266–67, it will tie up at Berlin, N.H., after a hundred-mile run. Hind-end brakeman holds tight to ladder rung and window bars of B&M "homey wooden caboose" riding on passenger-car trucks. Photo by PHILIP R. HASTINGS

PAGE 47. Extra 4007, Portland-Worcester, slams through Bleachery (Lowell), Mass., with appropriate steam and sound accompaniment. Head-end man "looks 'em over" as Coffin feedwater-hooded 4007 hauls out of the curve. Track gang observes this fine action scene nonchalantly. Photo by DONALD S. ROBINSON

PAGE 48. Detail of Pennsy boxcar shows sources of "Freight Train Troubles." Coupler release is a lever of different design from type described by author (see illustration, page 34).

PAGE 54. B&M hopper No. 8012, trailed by tank cars and a box, coasts into car retarders in East Somerville hump yard. "High Line" embankment at right. Photo from NEW ENGLAND RAIL SERVICE, Keene, N.H.

PAGE 58. K-8 No. 2688 hauls westbound freight train through grade crossing at Waltham Highlands, Mass. Gate tender wears clothing appropriate for a mid-March day in 1950. DONALD S. ROBINSON photo

PAGE 59. Four open platform, truss-rodded cars trail behind rebuilt Atlantic No. 3227 on a Boston–Lawrence express photographed at speed probably between Oak Grove and Wyoming, Mass. Railroad Photographs, from EDAVILLE MUSEUM collection

PAGE 62. Train No. 2537 will proceed into tunnel following a scheduled stop at the long since vanished medieval-style station at Salem, Mass. Somebody better line the iron? No need to, that's a spring switch just forward of engine No. 3626's pilot. View is from atop the tunnel portal, early '50s. Photo by DONALD S. ROBINSON

PAGE 64. With exhaust billowing skyward from stacks, pops and booster, engine No. 4009 hauls her tonnage through Rockingham Jct., N.H. H. W. Pontin collection of the 470 RAILROAD CLUB, Portland Division, RRE

PAGE 76. Passenger extra No. 3713 east ("last steam train" excursion) high-wheels onto bridge at Dover, N.H., headed by one of five Lima-built P-4a Class Pacifics, vintage 1934. B&M extra trains were identified by the engine number. DONALD S. ROBINSON photo

PAGE 81. Train No. 77 headed by 4-6-2 Pacific No. 3646 is poised just clear of the diamond at White River Jct. while predeparture station-platform bustle occurs alongside. Photo by DONALD S. ROBINSON

PAGE 85. Photo from NEW ENGLAND RAIL SERVICE, Keene, N.H.

PAGES 90–91. P-2 Pacifics and commuter trains at the North Station. A last look, through the camera of DONALD S. ROBINSON

PAGE 92. Drawbridges over Charles River, where tracks fan out into the North Station terminal. Mogul 1468 is at the head end of inbound local 3408. Note jack mounted at end of platform in foreground. Photo by DONALD S. ROBINSON

PAGE 93. Photo by PHILIP R. HASTINGS

PAGE 94, top. No. 4103, beautiful Baldwin-built Mountain type, pictured sanding up at East Deerfield for a time freight through to Rotterdam Jct., N.Y., 1948. EDGAR T. MEAD photo. Center: No. 3629 came to B&M in a batch of forty from Alco. Bottom: The 3700 at Billerica Shop in May, 1949 (see also text, p. 32). Last two from EDAVILLE MUSEUM

PAGE 97. NEW ENGLAND RAIL SERVICE photo

PAGE 99. Typical of B&M engine fittings were the handrails continuous from boiler top down smokebox front to pilot beam. Engines 3648 and 3658 in the North Station, August, 1954. Photo from EDAVILLE MUSEUM

PAGE 101. Engine No. 1003, typical of 4–4–0's that hauled passenger trains through the back yards and bushes of suburbia on branch lines. From EDAVILLE MUSEUM collection

PAGE 102. T-1a Class Berkshire No. 4014 was ten years old when snapped in action at Rigby on the Ides of March, 1938. Photo from EDAVILLE MUSEUM collection

PAGE 103. Diesel unit No. 4207 pilots A-B-A lashup and train past Tower 1, Rigby Yard. Photo by HERMAN SHANER

PAGE 107. That white stuff plastering roof, coupler and blade of B&M plow No. W3689 is from a 1948 winter snowfall. During a lull between bucking drifts, extra 1438 was photographed at Ayer by DONALD S. ROBINSON

PAGE 108. MP-4 derailed at Shelburne Falls, Mass., on October 11, 1954, and the job of getting things straightened out is in hand. Overturned car in left foreground offers fine view of underbody details described in chapter on "Freight Train Troubles." DONALD S. ROBINSON photo

PAGE 111. Time seems to stand still in this view of Wilmington, Mass., terminal, in which the old wooden water tower broods over engine house, Mogul 1441 on turntable, engineer in cab window, conductor and coaches—all under an overcast April sky that imparts a near-ghostly quality to the 1952 scene. One of the "things we won't experience again," except as fortuitously preserved on film by DONALD S. ROBINSON.

VANISHING MARKERS

The first engine I worked behind

. . . . But Not Forgotten

LOOKING BACK TO MY YEARS OF RAILROADING ON THE BOSTON & MAINE BRINGS FOND memories. During the late 1940s and early '50s I was a freight brakeman on the New Hampshire Division out of Mystic Junction, although working jobs on all divisions now and then. I worked in both freight and passenger service, as well as on work trains, flagging on light-engine moves, and switching in Boston yards.

Some people writing about railroads seem to hammer away at things like the fast streamliners, the great terminals, the breathtaking scenery, the wrecks and floods, statistics and the financial and political hanky-panky. These are fine to read about, but have no place in my memories except as things that might effect whatever job I was on. We always thought of the trains we worked on as "jobs."

A look at the old rule book or employees' timetables I've saved brings back the memories as vivid as ever—of riding night freights with a galloping, blasting 4100 on the head end; or the days and nights on steam switchers with their

9

bucking, rolling motions; and the buggies, not only the homey wooden ones but the newer steel ones.

Names come back to mind, too: Arthur Perkins, Superintendent of New Hampshire Division; Charles Came, Supt. of Portland Division; Walter Barrett, Supt. of Terminal Division. Then there were the trainmasters: McGuane, Brackett, Maloy, Richardson, Cate and Rourke—and B&M President Edward French himself, of fond memory.

I can recall as clear as yesterday—

—The first engine I worked behind, the 3715 *Kwasind,* a P-4 4–6–2, one of the few B&M engines with names.

—The clouds of steam surrounding the engines of commuter trains on frosty mornings.

—The homey smell of kerosene burning in the switchstand lanterns.

—The reflection of red and green signals on steel rails.

—The telegraph sounder clacking away in stations and yard offices, and the Prince Edward tobacco-can resonators the operators always stuck behind the sounders.

—The smell of soft coal smoke.

—The whine of steam turbo-generators providing current for headlights.

—The growl of a diesel way back in the night when I was out flagging a stalled freight.

—The "wham-wham-wham-wham" of slack shaking out of a string of box cars.

—The marker lights of passing trains, watching them get smaller and smaller back down the track, then flick out around a curve, or just disappear in the night.

I have to write about railroading in the words we used on the job, because that's the way I still think about it. About how we hardly ever uncoupled cars but "pulled the pin" or "got the pin" or "made a cut." To put on the brakes the engineer "went for the air" or "pinched 'em down," while, on the caboose, we could do the same thing by "pulling the air": apply brakes, that is, by opening a valve connected to the train line. We'd "get the iron" more often than "throw a switch." On the B&M, the direction of a train was either "inward" or "outward," depending on whether the train was headed toward or away from Boston. However, on the job we'd say "northbound," "eastbound" and so forth, instead.

I suppose there were some terms in railroad talk used on all railroads, like "iron" for "track," and "motion," meaning to signal with hands or a lamp to direct a train movement. But the B&M had its own common usage. Take the word "caboose" as an example. I've seen glossaries of railroad slang giving a dozen words for it; we almost always called it the "buggy"—occasionally the "hack" or the "clown's tent"—and that little structure on top, the cupola, was always the "monitor." I think the following goes for all New England, too, but on the B&M, anyway, we had engines rather than locomotives.❋

❋ ENGINE—A unit propelled by any form of energy, or a combination of such units operated from a single control, used in train or yard service.—*Rules for the Government of the Operating Department,* Boston and Maine Railroad, April, 1948.

Other B&M usage I'll try to make clear as we go along, as being fair to readers who've never worked on a railroad, but I'll cram as much as I can into the head end of this book, hoping that the hind end will read that much easier. Just to make sure, there's a glossary and an engine roster coupled on at the end.

Of course, it's more than twenty years now since these things happened to me. But times have changed, and railroading, too, I know. Maybe my book will be valuable as a record of railroad things once seen and done, but gone like those vanishing markers way down the track behind.

. . . clouds of steam surrounding the engines of commuter trains . . .

Railroad talk

2

Rule 99

Of all the rules laid down in the *Rules for the Government of the Operating Department* the most important, so far as the trainmen were concerned, was Rule 99. Under the protection of this rule all manner of things could be done. Reference to Rule 99 appears in many places in the rule book. It reads:

"When a train is moving under circumstances in which it may be overtaken by another train, the flagman must throw off lighted fusees at proper intervals and take such other action as necessary to insure full protection.

12

"When a train stops under circumstances in which it may be over-taken by another train, the flagman must go back immediately with flagman's signals a sufficient distance to insure full protection, placing two torpedoes and, when necessary, in addition, displaying lighted fusees. When recalled, and safety to the train will permit, he may re-turn, leaving the torpedoes and a lighted fusee."

Out on the line, this throwing off lighted fusees "at proper intervals" was a matter of experience and luck. We didn't just light one and heave it out; that way there was no telling where it might end up. The proper way to do it was to lean over the rear end and hold the lighted fusee with the spike end pointing forward and downward at about forty-five degrees, then drop it. One stood a good chance of spiking it right up in a tie. If it didn't "spike up" at least it wouldn't bounce far. Done with care, one's luck in spiking 'em up was better than 50 per cent. The idea was to get a fusee planted in time to provide some protection in case the train did stop and the flagman would have to go back.

A funny incident I remember had to do with dropping off fusees. Some of the old wooden buggies had sinks with old-fashioned straight drain pipes. One of the gang, a qualified conductor, discovered that a fusee would go right through one of these drains onto the track. He thought this was a clever way of dropping fusees from a moving train without having to go outside. He was conductor one night when I was flagging a Portland-Worcester extra. We began to slow down somewhere along the line, so I grabbed a fusee and started out the rear door.

"Look, I've got a better way," he said, taking the fusee. He lit it and dropped it into the sink drain. What he didn't know was that this drain had a dent in it, so that the fusee didn't drop through but got stuck instead. Smoke and gas came boiling up out of the sink drain as he madly dumped water down, trying to put out the fusee before it melted the pipe and set fire to the car. (It's almost impos-sible to put a fusee out with water. I've seen them burn under water.) Somehow he kept it from burning up the buggy, but it was nearly impossible to breathe in there. I grabbed my flagging gear and beat it out the rear, because we were slowing to a stop. That was the end of the clever trick, for that night anyway.

When going back to flag, especially in Automatic Block Signal territory, we often did not place torpedoes—"guns," we called them—if we knew that the stop was going to be for a short time only. There was no need to hold up trains com-ing along later under a clear signal indication. However, in *non*-signal territory it was a different story. We placed the guns and left them there. Usually, the non-signal territory meant the branch lines. Some of the branches, such as the Lexington Branch and the Central Massachusetts, had First Class trains (pas-senger trains) that had to be protected against as per Rule 99, and no nonsense about it. The local freights on those branches got orders which stated, in part, "not protecting against extra trains." But, if we got onto the time of a First Class train, protection had to be full and absolute.

From time to time the Sperry Rail Testing car operated over our lines. Testing speed was about ten miles per hour, with frequent stops. The section foreman in whose district the car was moving trailed along on his motor section car a few car lengths behind, in order to learn what defects were found and what he had to do about them. The flagman usually rode on that section car so that he was handy for the frequent stops. The stops were of short duration, just a couple of minutes, and we'd be off again.

I was flagging just such an outfit one day, running from Lowell to Boston. At Wilmington we stopped, and I got off the section car with a flag. A trainmaster was standing there watching things. When we backed off in Wilmington to clear a passenger train he got ahold of me.

"What are you supposed to be doing?" he asked.

"Flagging," I answered.

"Where are the torpedoes?" he wanted to know.

"We only stop for such a short time I didn't think they were necessary," I said.

"Read Rule 99 and flag by the book if you want to stay around here," was what I got back.

OK. By the book.

We stayed at Wilmington for lunch and then took off for Boston with me loaded to the gills with fusees and torpedoes. As usual, we stopped many times. Each time I left two guns behind. We got as far as Walnut Hill, where we had to back off for No. 316, an express train from Concord.*

We waited. Came time for No. 316. Nothing in sight. Conductor was pacing. Wonder where they are? Still waiting. 316 must be late. Then we began to hear the cannonading. They must have hit eight or ten sets of torpedoes between Wilmington and Walnut Hill. They came into sight just crawling along, train crew hanging out of every door. Their conductor was wild—not to mention that ours was pretty worked up, too.

"What's the idea of using all those guns?" he yelled.

"You heard the trainmaster up at Wilmington," was my reply. "Railroad by the book is the name of the game."

When we went along it was "modified flagging" from there to Boston.

In flagging behind a train in Automatic Block Signal territory it was only necessary to protect against trains running at restricted speed. However, when flagging wreckers or work trains that could foul tracks other than the track they were on, the flagging had to be deep and protect well, especially on the unoccupied, or "hot" iron.

The rule in the employee's timecard† reads, in part:

"Flagmen must go out in accordance with instructions of the Conduc-

---

* Concord, New Hampshire, always in this book, unless otherwise identified.   † Timetable.

tor or Yard Foreman and in full compliance with Rule 99, placing torpedoes. They will permit no train or engine to pass until it is first stopped and fully advised as to the presence and location of work equipment, unless called in by whistle recall signal or on personal advice of the Conductor or Yard Foreman that the line is clear for safe passage.

"They must definitely know the whistle recall signal was sounded by their equipment before withdrawing flag for passage of train . . ."

Here is what can happen: I was on the crew of a work train working south out of Wilmington. We had the usual line-up of equipment, a self-propelled crane and a couple of ballast cars. We were on the outward main down around North Woburn Junction and had swung the boom out over the inward main, thus fouling it.

It seems that on this same day the Interstate Commerce Commission (ICC) and other interested parties were running a brake test of some kind. They had three or four coaches fitted out with some kind of instrumentation, a diesel on the head end, and were running extra. They had made their run from Boston to Lowell in the morning and were due to come back to Boston right after noon-time. When they had gone north we were still in Wilmington Yard, where our conductor was warned not to hold them up on the return trip.

After lunch in Wilmington our outfit got ready to go on down to North Woburn Junction, but there was no word yet of the extra coming out of Lowell. So they left me at Wilmington to flag the "hot" iron and moved off down the outward main. Conductor said he'd call me in when the extra left Lowell. I walked up around the curve, put down guns, and came back to Wilmington.

In due time the extra left Lowell and came flying southward on the inward main, running their brake tests. If our conductor was aware of the extra's approach and called me in I never heard it. (The horns on those cranes were kind of weak.) Next thing I knew the extra was whistling up around Silver Lake, and then they got my torpedoes. Fancy extra or not, I cracked off a fusee and—at last—they went for the air. They sailed by me a whole train length before stopping in a cloud of dust.

Officials came out of everywhere. Ignoring the whole crowd, I ran up to the head end and told the engineer about the work train and to look sharp for a motion when he hauled down there. Trainmaster was demanding to know why I stopped them. I told him I didn't hear my train call me in so that I was cleared according to Rule 99. Then I wanted to know why they didn't shut off when they got my guns. I got no answer to that one.

Another example of hot-iron flagging would be when a train stopped on "emergency air" for some reason unknown to the head end. In that case the head-end man was required to beat it up ahead and flag the opposite main against opposing trains. There was no way of knowing, but perhaps a derailment back there had spilled cars all over both tracks, which *has* happened. Symbol freight BW-1 was stopped this way one night, the air going into emergency. To learn what happened, the conductor hiked along the train and what he found was—a tank car lying on its side in the middle of the *other* main line. So there was plenty of reason for the flagging ahead rule.

Unless relieved of flagging by a "not protecting" order giving us exclusive rights, or working within Yard Limits, we had to protect as per Rule 99. We *always* had to protect against First Class trains, no matter where we were. Back we'd go, "with flagman's signals," which consisted of:

Day Signals: a red flag, torpedoes and fusees.

Night Signals: a red light, a white light, torpedoes and fusees.

All has since been changed; they don't go flagging with a red light any more. Strange railroading these days.

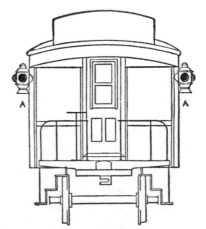

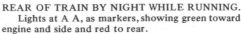

REAR OF TRAIN BY NIGHT WHILE RUNNING.
Lights at A A, as markers, showing green toward
engine and side and red to rear.

Ball signal, Waumbek Junction, N. H.

3   Signals

I'D BETTER BRING IN THE SUBJECT OF SIGNALS NOW, BECAUSE THEY FIGURE STRONG IN what's to come, and we had a lot more to do with them than just admire their pretty reflections on the tracks.

Eighty-eight out of 245 pages in the Rule Book are about signals, with pictures in color showing them as we would see them from the head end, seventy-five different ones in all. The B&M had a full assortment, from the most modern Centralized Train Control (CTC) systems to the very early ball type signals.

As late as 1934 there were quite a number of these old ball signals scattered around the B&M, in New Hampshire at Manchester, Rochester, Elmwood, Whitefield, Berlin, Epping and Waumbeck Junction, also three at Nashua, two at Concord and Hooksett. In Vermont there was one each at White River Junction, Wells River, Bellows Falls, Brattleboro and North Bennington; in Massachusetts, at Winchendon. There was one also just north of the Portland Union Station, but this was on the Maine Central. By the time I began railroading in the late '40s their numbers had diminished; I remember only those at Bellows Falls, Concord, White River and Nashua.

Remote electrical control was never applied to these ball devices. One or more of the balls would be hauled by hand to the top of a pole for a "Clear"

17

indication. On some of them a hook was provided under the ball for hanging an oil lantern at night, or an arrangement of lights was mounted on the pole so that the indication could be seen at night as well as by day.

At one time, the most common type of signal was the two position "home" and "distant" Automatic Block Signal. In the '40s these were still to be found on the branch lines, such as the Gloucester Branch and the Saugus Branch, and also between Concord and White River, Concord and Plymouth (N.H.), and some other locations where the traffic was not too heavy. The sketch shows this signal and the three indications that were possible:

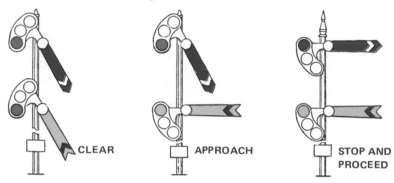

The "Clear" indication speaks for itself and the "Stop and Proceed" meant exactly those two moves; we'd make what was called a "know nothing" stop at this indication, then haul along at restricted speed prepared to stop short of a train or obstruction. The "Approach" allowed us to move along, but on the alert, and sometimes, when following a slow moving train through many blocks "Yellow for Yellow," one could be lulled into trouble. You expect the next block to be Yellow; suddenly there's a Red one—and just beyond it a pair of marker lights.

Originally these signals had kerosene lamps. In later years they were electrified, the lights becoming much brighter. Many times, in the dark and lonely stretches of the north country, these lights were a welcome sight. Their reliability was unquestioned. We had no vandalism problems, but I doubt whether these things would live a week in urban areas now.

On heavier traffic lines, where trains were faster and perhaps closer together, Color Light Signals were installed. The two-light signals gave an extra indication, as shown below:

They were very brilliant, like searchlights, for daytime viewing. At night they reflected off shiny rails in a grand manner. This type is in use now. They were installed on the main lines between Boston and Mechanicville (N.Y.), Concord, Portland and Portsmouth, as well as the Worcester-Ayer line, the Stoney Brook and Lowell Junction Branches. They were "approach lighted," that is, they remained dark until the train hit the block ahead of them. Then they'd blink on.

Below is a signal that we called a "Stagger Block." It was the signal next in advance of a Home Signal. It was capable of showing the same indications as the Color Light Signals:

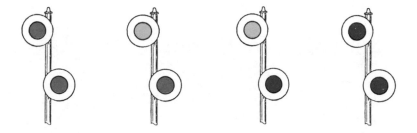

The Home Signals were always at a location where there were diverging routes. These would be at junctions such as Wakefield or North Chelmsford or Ayer; or at crossovers such as at Graniteville and Kennebunk; or at the entrance to a yard such as at South Lowell or Concord. They were almost always part of an interlocking system, or plant, controlled from a nearby tower or by a CTC system, the operator of which might be in a dispatcher's office miles away. The plant at North Billerica was controlled by electric locks in trackside boxes, and could only be operated after calling the dispatcher in Concord. The picture below shows the indications and the names we gave them:

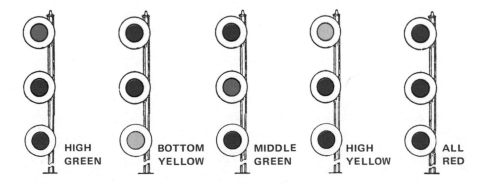

HIGH GREEN   BOTTOM YELLOW   MIDDLE GREEN   HIGH YELLOW   ALL RED

The type of signal shown above was also called a "three-arm pole," because Home Signals originally had semaphore arms. These older signals were operated by levers in a nearby tower through rods and pull wires rigged about a foot off the ground. These were great things for brakemen to get tangled up with in the dark, and many a skun shin or worse resulted from encounters with them. When I was railroading the only such installations left that I saw were at Bleachery and Hale Street in Lowell, and at North Chelmsford. The drawing shows the type:

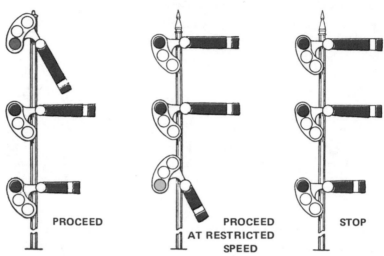

PROCEED   PROCEED   STOP
             AT RESTRICTED
                SPEED

By the late '40s Color Light Signals had replaced the semaphore arms, but the name "three-arm pole" stuck. I'm told that years ago, when Boston yard had this type of signal, there was one outside the North Station that had so many arms and could indicate so many moves that it was called the "curiosity pole," there were so many people looking for it.

Plentiful around the yards in Boston and other terminals was the little dwarf type signal we called a "jack," indicating Red, Green or Yellow, as conditions called for:

Then there were Pot Signals mounted on the masts at hand-thrown switches, which would revolve to show an indication whenever a switch was thrown. In my time these were lighted by oil lamps, but they have become such easy pickings for vandals that reflectors are used now instead:

Rods and pull wires rigged about a foot off the ground . . . Many a skun shin or worse resulted from encounters with them.

In addition to the regular pole signals described above there were signals mounted on gantries over the tracks or on brackets attached to the poles, and special signals too numerous to take up space describing. Very important, however, were the Train Order Signals at stations and interlocking plants located all over the B&M system. Here's what they looked like; we thought they had a real New England look:

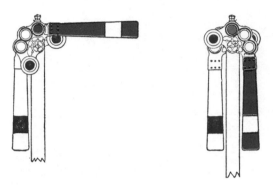

Without going into detail about how the Train Order Signals were used as manual block signals, let me say that a "Stop" indication showing on one of these meant exactly that: Stop, for orders from the dispatcher. However, to avoid delay, these could be "hooped up" to us on the fly, in which case the operator would be out making a "Come ahead" motion with a yellow lamp. We'd grab the orders—so-called "19" orders—from a hand-held hoop or from a fork mounted on a post at trackside, without stopping the train. Many times this happened to me at Franklin or Halcyon or Canaan.

Though not exactly signals, there were also signposts or "boards" along the track that we had to pay attention to. In fact, "the board" is what we'd often say when referring to signal indications of any kind, as well as to mean the call board in yard offices where we marked up our names to be called for work.

The real New England look

Color Light Signals loom over this meet at Ayer, Mass.

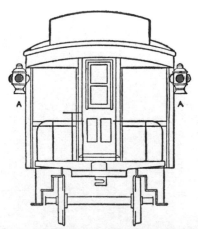

REAR OF TRAIN BY NIGHT WHEN ON SIDING
TO BE PASSED BY ANOTHER TRAIN.
Lights at A A, as markers, showing green to side
and rear.

Most of the head brakeman's work was on the ground.

Head End

I WAS FORTUNATE TO HAVE RAILROADED BEFORE THE STEAM ENGINES DISAPPEARED off the B&M roster. My function as head-end brakeman didn't involve actual operation of those old-timers, but I covered enough jobs from a cab deck to remember how it was to ride in a cab and how the engineers and firemen earned their pay. There wasn't any rule said I had to shovel coal, but I'd do it when some extra muscle on a scoop would help get a job over the line.

The small switchers, 0–6–0 G-11's, were powerful little critters but—as any switcher is bound to be—rough-riding engines. On a main-line move, once they got going, it was either hang on tight or get bounced off the front edge of the fireman's seat, which is where the head brakeman perched. The G-11's could squirm over any kind of rough trackage in cramped industrial sidings, but their contortions were such that one never rode in the gangway, a bad place to be in case of a derailment. You might be trapped between the cab and the tender. I had a great uncle who was crushed to death that way.

These G-11's were used on almost all the local freights out of Boston. An exception was the West Medford job, where a big 0–8–0 switcher was used instead. I never knew for sure why, unless that big an engine was needed because of its water capacity. There weren't any water plugs at either West Medford or North Somerville—at which places this job spent the day—so the engines had to run all day on water taken on at Boston.

A few jobs had Moguls: the "BB" Bedford local, the Hillsboro, the Ayer. These trains made long main-line runs where the faster 2–6–0 was better than a jerky, swaying 0–6–0. At one time after 1900 the Moguls were the standard passenger and freight engines on the B&M; they were still used extensively during the late '40s, replacing the old 4–4–0's in local passenger service (and were themselves replaced, by P-2 Pacifics, as they got older and their boiler tubes wore out). However, on local freights with much switching to be done, the Moguls had a particular disadvantage—their old-fashioned "Johnson Bar" reverse gear.

Those Johnson Bars were mean things. If not handled just right, they could put you through the cab wall. Sometimes it took a two-man heave to throw them over. I recall one Johnson Bar incident in particular:

We were at Billerica✳ Shop on the BB local, just about ready to come into Boston. We had switched over onto our train and were looking for a motion to haul down to the main line. We saw a lantern say "Back up," so the engineer horsed her over and we started to shove back. But then a "Stop" motion. Then "Ahead slow." Then "Back up." Then "Stop." After a few more motions of this kind, each time a struggle with the Johnson Bar, the engineer said, "For Pete's sake, go back and see what's going on." I went and found that the boys on the hind end were cutting wood for the buggy stove by putting sticks on the rail and running the buggy back and forth over them. I didn't tell that to the engineer; I'm sure he'd have gone back, too, with a coal maul—and not to cut wood with either! I told him they were trying to make a hitch with a bad knuckle.

All engines had injectors to force water into the boiler; the big ones, in addition, had steam feedwater pumps to help out. The injectors were usually placed in the cab, one on each side of the boiler, though some engines (the Moguls, as I recollect) had the "waterworks" across the boiler back head. There was a trick to getting those injectors going. You had to pull the lever back slowly, listening and "feeling." You could tell when it "caught" from the solid "click" sound and touch. If it didn't catch, the water wouldn't go into the boiler. Steam blew back into the water lines instead. It was necessary to get that water into the boiler and *not* on a bare crown sheet,† or the results would be spectacular and very likely injurious.

✳ Pronounced " 'Bill-rick'-a."   † Top of firebox.

Water plug

No. 452 0-6-0 in storage at Boston, 1955

No more West Medford local for aged 0-8-0 No. 651

No. 1488, one of the rare Moguls with footboards

As we pulled out of Boston one morning, the fireman went to put the water on. "I'll run the water!" shouted the engineer. OK, he'll run the water, and on we went. Somewhere up around Melrose I looked at the water glass, but couldn't see any water. I nudged the fireman and said, "Is he running the water for sure?" Fireman took a look and yelled over to the engineer about low water. Engineer never even looked at the gage but went for the injector—and I went for the gangway. Not that I was any better off there, but if the boiler was going to blow I didn't want to make a hole in the cab on my way out. It didn't blow, or I wouldn't be writing this. But there were some hairy moments until the water did show back in the glass. After that, the engine crew had a good understanding about who would run the water.

At night, another time, we were leaving Billerica Shop, heading south on the BB pulled by the usual Mogul. The waterworks had been performing all right during the day. Now, every time the engineer opened the throttle, the water disappeared out of the glass. Close the throttle, the water came back. Once again I felt that the gangway was a good place to be. They got it straightened out—I never knew how—and it behaved OK from there to Boston.

If an engine's safety valve—pop valve—started to lift, you could stop it by putting on the water. You could overdo it, of course, and get her too full. Then she'd suck up water and fill the cylinders, knocking out a cylinder head if the cylinder cocks weren't opened soon enough. You could tell when an engine was full of water from the slushy sound of the exhaust up the stack. Anyone standing around with a white shirt on could throw it away tomorrow, because engines full of water caused liquid soot to fall far and wide.

Although most of the head brakeman's work was on the ground, we would do a little extra on the engine, too. We used to take on water and shovel coal off the pile over to where it was handy for the fireman. He in turn would pull the head pin for us and set up hand brakes on the head cars of a long train, as we were required to do coming in to Mystic Junction with a drag of fifty or more cars. This kind of assist saved brakemen a lot of walking.

On engines with stokers we had to drag metal slides over the stoker pit as the coal pile in the tender was depleted. This required digging around to clear the slide, then getting ahold of the slide with a hook and jerking it forward. Chunks of coal off the pile would then tumble into the space just opened up. That is, they would if the coal wasn't frozen. Then we'd have to get in there with a coal maul and "mine" coal until it flowed.

On a freight job one night, Boston to Worcester (BW-1), the coal pile froze, so that somewhere around Clinton I started mining. I worked away at this back there in the dark, breaking up coal and nudging it down into the stoker worm. It was one of those biting cold nights when the exhaust steam turns to dense clouds and rolls right back into the coal pit. We had a heavy train; the stoker was running constantly, and it was all I could do to keep the coal moving into it.

When we finally topped Break-Neck Hill at West Boylston, the fireman came back and pulled me out of the coal pile. I had dug a cavern right into it! It took the two of us with slice bars to knock it down. We made it into Worcester about midnight, but it was four in the morning before the remaining pile was thawed out enough to put more coal in. Sure, it froze again on the way back to Boston.

For some reason, when we got bad coal, it always seemed to be at Worcester. I've seen coal full of dirt, pieces of brake shoes and other junk. A piece of something got jammed in the stoker worm once, then it wound a coal maul right in after it and stopped the whole works.

With steam engines there was the problem of smoke. An engine whose fire was burning right showed little or no smoke at the stack. Most of what was visible was exhaust steam which, in cold weather, condensed into white clouds. These would disappear soon, but smoke would hang in the air longer. Smoke is the result of incomplete combustion, and is composed of unburned carbon. Engines that make a lot of smoke are not running efficiently, and that is frowned upon from on high.*

Any engine would smoke when the fireman was bailing in coal, because the raw coal "cooled" the fire for an instant, making smoke which would quickly disappear once the raw coal caught fire. As long as a good draft was being drawn through the firebox, complete combustion took place and little smoke was in evidence. If the blower was on, or the engine was working steam, the required draft was present; but if the blower was *not* on and the engineer shut off the throttle, then the draft quit and black smoke rolled forth. If a fireman was on the job, he'd cut in the blower a little as soon as the engineer shut off. One could hear this take place, especially on passenger trains approaching station stops.

On an engine that was steaming properly, steam pressure went up when the engineer shut off. Putting the blower on (to cut the smoke) kept the fire hot, so that steam pressure quickly got to the blow-off point. To come sailing into a station with the pops roaring not only caused a lot of racket, but wasted steam which could be better used in moving the engine. To keep the pressure down the fireman would crack the firebox doors open a notch. This allowed the blower to draw air in over the fire, burning up the smoke but not fanning the fire too hot.

Another stunt was to put on water with one of the injectors, provided the boiler wasn't too full already. This would knock down the pressure and keep the pops from lifting. However it was done, the smoke had to be abated.

If an engine crew habitually made smoke, there was bound to be a complaint. Out would come the smoke inspector to investigate—in my time, a gentleman

---

* Rule 942: They (firemen) must fire their engine, as far as possible, in such a manner as to avoid the emission of black smoke, especially near residential sections of towns and cities. . . .

known to us as "Three-fingered Jack." He'd watch the offending job for a few days, then warn the crew about making black smoke. Though it was the fireman's job to control the smoke, it was the engineer's responsibility to see that he did it.

Stoker-fired engines might be smokers like any others, but they were also cinder throwers. Cinders were fused particles of incompletely burned coal sucked through the tubes and up the stack, there to rain down far and wide and drift into eyes and ears. Stokers pulverized coal so fine that much of what went into the firebox fused and kept traveling on out the stack. The K-8 2–8–0 types were the champion cinder throwers.

Properly steaming engines burned their coal completely, making little smoke. Others, perhaps "drafted wrong" to begin with, could break a fireman's back trying to keep them hot. Lots of smoke, but no heat. And there were other engine ailments to contend with. Once on the Portland job we had a 4000 Class Berkshire that dropped arch bricks. Now an arch is that structure built of fire brick inside the firebox that causes the fire and hot gasses first to double back toward the fire door, then up and forward under the crown sheet, then into and through the tubes. The fire bricks are hefty things and, on this particular 4000, they kept dropping out of the arch into the fire. Whenever one fell it formed a

One of the champion cinder throwers

king-size clinker which, of course, wouldn't burn. The fireman and I worked half the night breaking up clinkers hotter than Hell's brimstone and fishing them out through the fire door. The engine wouldn't steam; it just bogged us down even with the stoker going most of the time. I shoveled over so much coal and pulled so many slides that by the time we got to Rigby I was way at the back of the coal pit. As soon as the engine limped into the house at Rigby, they killed the fire and put in a new arch. We had her out that same night on the return trip. Before we got to Boston a couple more bricks fell, but we got in without *too* much trouble.

Whenever there was a main-line move made with a light engine,* a flagman had to go along. I was called quite often for this kind of job, from Boston to Billerica Shop and back. We'd go over to the "Big House," the Somerville engine terminal, for the engine we were to take. We'd stick a red flag in the rear coupler knuckle or hang a red lantern on the back of the tank. With an OK from the dispatcher, off we'd go. The return trip, we'd usually have a newly shopped engine. It would be all painted up, looking like new. Not a knock or a clank out of the running gear. We were some proud coming down through Winchester with a fancied-up P-3 or P-2, or a 4100.

Once, when I was called for a light engine job, it turned out to be one engine on steam towing a dead 0–6–0 switcher. We started out all right, with me riding the dead one. We hadn't progressed as far as the High Line† when the switcher's cab became full of flying ashes. I couldn't see because my eyes were full of ashes, and I couldn't get the attention of the head end. I groped around and found that the throttle had been left partly open, but I couldn't close it. I was some dirty! At last, by opening the fire door wide I stopped that ash cloud from blowing out of the fire box. Why this trick worked I never could find out.

Another time, on a similar call, the job was to tow a small paper mill switch engine from the shop to Concord, and deadhead home. They gave us a long-legged 3700 passenger engine to do the towing. When we saw the little thing that we were to tow we couldn't believe it; it was no bigger than the tender of the 3700.

When we were all set the shop gave us their blessing, and we backed down to the main line. I rode the little one. Once cleared for the main line we took off, the high-wheel passenger engine just loping along but the little drivers of the switcher churning around some fast. It was this way to Lowell, where we were stopped by signals. The engineer felt around the switcher and found, as a matter of course, that every pin and bearing was hot. He poured on oil and we moved along. After four miles or so we stopped for another check, and things were hot again. This is the way it went; finally we were stopping every two miles. The dispatcher was going nuts! We were moving so slow that we had to put into

---

* An engine and tender all by their lonesome. † Overpass at Mystic Junction (see map).

Another mudsucker!

every side track to let traffic by. We'd hoped to arrive at Concord in time to deadhead home on No. 24 that same day. Instead, we wound up on the milk train, getting in at Boston after midnight.

Here's another light-engine tow job I'll never forget. At the engine house we found that the towing engine was an old 2900, one of the series we called "mud-suckers," and that we'd be pulling a dead P-2.

I rode the mudsucker this time, because the weather was cold and so was the P-2. The engine crew figured that if we hurried right along we might get back in time to cover another job the same day, so away we went. We flew up the main line like an express train, probably a lot faster than a light engine was supposed to go, and certainly faster than we were supposed to tow a dead engine with the main rods connected. The way we went around the curve at Montvale was something to be admired.

Presently we arrived at North Billerica where we had to shove back through a crossover and down to the shop. Some shop men waiting at North Billerica station asked if they could hitch a ride to the shop. "Sure, climb into that dead P-2." Now pushing the old girl, we backed down toward the shop. At the shop switch we reversed direction again, heading up into the yard. Something went haywire! The engineer yelled, "She's going over!" Over she went, indeed. The firemen and I were knocking each other out trying to climb the coal pile. In a very short time that old mudsucker Santa Fe type was almost two-thirds on her side. The tank* was on the ground, but upright, and the P-2 had stopped just short of the

* Tender.

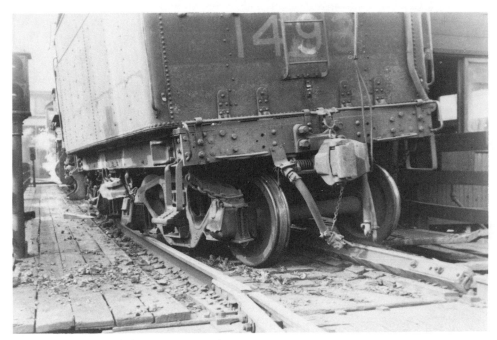

The tank was on the ground, but upright.

torn-up rails and so stood with her feet on the iron. Rails were wound up into the mudsucker's running gear like horseshoe nails. When the gang in the P-2 saw what was happening, they flew out of that engine like birds. I never saw men vacate an engine so fast.

There was no steam blowing in the mudsucker's cab, but the water lines to the tender were torn off; so they killed the fire. Water was running all over the place. We discovered that the flanges on the lead truck were as sharp as a knife blade and had split open a switch, putting us on the ground. I couldn't help thinking how we had gone flying around that curve at Montvale, and through other switches as well!

It was the last run for that particular Santa Fe. They brought out the hook* to heave her up and, later, cut her up for scrap.

Another call to flag on a light engine was to deadhead all the way to White River Junction, bring an engine back to Billerica Shop, then deadhead on home. I found the engine crew on the same train I caught, No. 305 to White River, and we hoped, if we got any kind of a break, to be home by supper time. Our job was in the engine house at Westboro, the station ahead of White River. Another 2900, another mudsucker! What it was doing there was beyond me; we figured it was hiding.

We got our orders, hung up white flags signifying we were running extra, and took right out for Billerica. Things looked good until we got to somewhere on

* Wrecking crane.

the hill between Lebanon and Mascoma—when the stoker quit. No amount of tinkering would get it going. All there was left to do was to hand-fire the thing.

Now to hand-fire a stoker-fed engine is somewhat of a stunt. The firebox itself is half the size of the living room at home. The fire door is too small and set too high, and the coal pile far away. Furthermore, a light engine is hard to keep hot because it doesn't work hard enough to keep a good draft going. Add to that an engine with other ills, not the least of which are a number of steam leaks, and you have some deal.

Well, we started hand-firing this old hen. When I say we, I mean that both the fireman and I went at it. Luckily, there was an extra scoop. I was in the coal pit heaving coal out on the deck and the fireman was putting it where it did the most good. We weren't keeping up with it, however. On down grades we gained a little, but not for long. The fire had holes you could push a wheelbarrow through. What wasn't holes was clinkers.

When we finally made Concord, nobody at the engine house there knew anything to do with the conked-out stoker. We tried to park the old girl there, but Concord would have no part of her. After blowing up the best fire we could, we started off again for Billerica. The day was getting older.

The dispatcher put us in out of the way of every train the B&M had. At last, long after suppertime, we wheezed through Lowell. Not too far now to the shop, and it was the last mile for that old 2900. When we moved off the main line at the shop, we'd had it. We crept up to the ash pit in the dark with just enough steam left to make it. As we walked away from the thing, the headlight generator had barely enough life to make the headlight glow an orange color—the final gasp for that old mudsucker. She was cut up with the rest.

Extra engines on trains were known as "helpers," or "pushers." A helper was an additional engine on the head end. A pusher was exactly that: an engine pushing behind the buggy. When a helper was working, the engineer of the second engine set the pace because it was easier for the man in the helper to hear the exhaust of the engine behind him than for the second man to hear the stack up front. Hearing the second engine's exhaust, the head engineer could work his engine accordingly, and share the load. However, the man on the head engine handled the air.

The B&M may have used helpers here and there, but I saw one used only once, on WB-2 from Worcester to Ayer. We really didn't need a helper that time; I think it was just a convenient way to get an engine to Ayer without calling another flagman.

Pushers were another story, however. We had lots of those. We'd have pushers from East Fitchburg up Ashburnham Hill to Gardner. We'd have pushers from East Deerfield to Gardner, from Worcester up through Greendale to West Boylston, and from White River up to Canaan.

Pushers were another story, however . . .

A pusher operation was something to behold. In the yard, the pusher—usually a K-8—would tie on behind and the air would be connected up to him. After the brake test, ready to go, the head end would whistle off. The pusher engineer would shove in all the slack* he could move and sit there with his throttle open. Then he'd whistle off and the head end would open up, taking cars off the top of the pile, so to speak. In short order the whole outfit was moving; by the time we went by the yard office the pusher would be really talking it up.

For anyone who likes "stack talk," the place to be is in a buggy with a K-8 pusher working behind. There isn't much said around the buggy at that time because nothing can be heard. After a few miles it comes as a relief when the pusher is cut off.

---

* Couplers and draft gear were constructed to allow some lateral play, or "slack," between cars coupled together. Cars being pulled would "stretch" the slack; cars being pushed would "bunch" it. Before starting a train, the engineer "shook out the slack" with a back up move causing the slack to bunch. Forward motion stretched the slack a car at time, progressively, through the train.

We used to cut the pusher off "on the fly." We had a long iron rod bent in such a way that we could reach down with it and close the angle cock on the rear of the buggy. When it was time to drop the pusher, we'd get out on the rear platform and carefully close the angle cock. Then we'd get the pin and motion the pusher engineer to shut off. This he'd do, and, when he dropped off, the air hose would part and his air would slow him down while we went on our way. It's best to be hanging on at a time like this because we know there'll be a lusty jerk when our slack runs out.

We had a pusher one night out of Worcester on WB-2, as we very often did. Things went well until up near Greendale. Then the pusher began to lag. It was an engine that wouldn't steam. We went slower and slower. We looked at the knuckles on the hind end and could see that they were stretched tight. Since it made no sense to pull both a heavy train *and* the pusher, we decided to cut him off. When we could manage to get the pin, we dropped him. About that time our engineer, who was a crotchety type, looked back and saw that the pusher was off. He decided that he wasn't going to do all the work, so he shut off too. That was the end of that. We "doubled" the hill✽ that night and were half the night doing it.

In the late '40s, diesels were beginning to show up in considerable numbers. Most of my experience with them was routine, but there are a few things about them that stay with me, which I'll tell even at the risk of alienating the steam fans.

The engines I worked on that impressed me most were the big GM Electromotive diesels, the FT's, B&M series 4200. What struck me first was that they rode like a Pullman car. They were cool in the summer, warm in winter. I must say that we kind of looked forward to working on them. In the cab there was an extra seat for the brakeman and, compared to steam, one found that diesels weren't at all noisy. In fact, a long night trip had a tendency to put one to sleep. Inward bound on UB-2 one night, we had three units. North of Concord the diesel engine in the lead unit conked out—a malfunction. But we had a light train, so we could roll along on the other two units and that was a really quiet ride.

The light-engine moves on diesels were usually from Boston to the shop, whenever wheels, bearings or other truck parts needed replacement. We'd leave Boston running forward to North Billerica, cross the road† there and back in on the Lexington Branch. We'd back down the branch through the woods to the shop switch near Bennett Hall. By heading down into the shop from this point, we were turned in the right direction both for the shop and for heading back to Boston.

✽ Take half the train uphill, put it in a siding, go back for the other half.
† To cross over from one main line to another, as from outward main to inward main.

This kind of job took only three-to-four hours. We'd run the engine or engines, if there was more than one unit, over one of the shop pits. After the maintainers had disconnected things, the shop crane would lift the engine bodies and swing them over onto new trucks already spotted accurately on the adjoining track. It was then a matter for the maintainers to connect everything up again. When they were finished, a shop crew started the engines and backed out to run them up and down the shop tracks, checking things out. When they were satisfied, they turned 'em over to us and we came back to Boston.

Routine stuff, as I said above, but I was impressed also by the way those diesels could pull. When the engineer latched one of those things open, something had to happen. Either he'd start the train or, if he wasn't careful, pull it apart!

I must say that we kind of looked forward to working on them.

Home-away-from-home for train crews laying over

5

Hind End

So MUCH HAS BEEN WRITTEN ABOUT THE CABOOSE, HOW IT WAS A HOME-AWAY-from-home for train crews laying over that I'll only say it was true, in my time, and remark in passing that in local service the buggy was merely a rolling office. The through jobs, of course, had buggies fitted out for sleeping and eating. They were, for the most part, kept clean, neat and well stocked.

At White River Junction, the buggy track was right next to the river, over beyond the rip track.* It was a gathering place for the crews from the New Hampshire Division, the Connecticut River and White Mountain jobs, as well as crews from Canadian Pacific trains. Life was rugged and simple, but very satisfying. We slept there, ate there, did our chores there, talked shop and spun yarns.

Every buggy had a potbellied stove, on which we did our cooking: steaks, chops, potatoes, bacon, eggs, stews—all of it good and hearty. We got coal for the stove out of a gondola attached to the wrecker over on the next track. Each buggy had an icebox that we'd keep supplied from an ice locker at the rip track. There were water cans to fill, and lamps to fill up with kerosene fetched from the rip-track shed. When all the supplies were on hand, we'd scrub the buggy floor and hang the mop on the roof ladder to dry. We had to clean all parts of the lanterns—lamps, chimneys and globes. Ordinarily there were four or five lamps in each car, two of which were on the conductor's desk. We had a pair of marker lights to clean and fill also. When we were getting ready to leave the River, the flagging equipment would be laid out. This consisted of fusees, torpedoes, red flag, and red and white hand lanterns. The markers were hung up, lighted if it was dark, showing red to the rear, green to the front and sides.

Once our train was made up, the switcher would come and get us and tie us onto the rear car. The car knocker† hooked up the air; then, when the engine pumped up the train line, the air gage in the buggy showed the pressure. The conductor came on with an armful of waybills. Also our orders, which the flagman had to "read and understand."** The head end "whistled off" two short blasts, the signal to start. The slack ran out, jerking the buggy into motion, and we'd ride the rear platform until over the Connecticut River bridge and past the

---

* Repair track.   † Car inspector.   ** Quoted from rule book.

Westboro engine house. Then we were fairly on our way to the sound of the wheels clacking over the rail joints.

This is the way we left White River one night when we had with us a student brakeman making his first trip on a through freight. We were all up in the monitor, me sitting on the left side, the conductor and the student on the right. Some time after we passed Canaan the conductor said to the student:

"We have a passenger train, No. 313, coming at us. Where are we going to meet him?"

The student got out his timecard and started to figure. Finally he said:

"We can meet him at Grafton."

As he said that, we were passing Grafton.

"Wow!" said the conductor, jumping up, "We just passed Grafton."

The student did what most of them do; he picked the next place.

"We'll go to Danbury," he said.

"Can't do that," says the conductor. "Siding won't hold all the cars we've got. Boy, we're in a fix now!"

I knew the conductor was pulling the kid's leg. Soon he hollered over to me:

"I think I'll get off. You going to stay on?"

I said I'd stay for a while because we were going pretty fast. Down out of the monitor went the kid and made for the rear door. I followed and grabbed him and asked what he was going to do.

"Get off," he said.

I asked him if he thought he could get off at forty miles an hour and he allowed that was maybe too fast to unload. Well, he calmed down in a few minutes and looked at his timecard again, and his watch, and finally figured we might be able to meet No. 313 at Gale. Of course, Gale was where we were going to make the meet anyway. As we started to slow down, the kid decided he was going to live after all. When we had hauled in and the iron had been lined,* the conductor said:

"Well, I think we should have two minutes of silent prayer."

At Concord, the student was ready to get off, deadhead back to White River and forget about road braking. I talked him out of it and suppose he eventually marked up his name on the White River board, but I never saw him again after we reached Boston.

One job of hind-end braking was when I nearly got mine. It was a night so cold I can't remember any worse. At Concord I walked up to the head end to help out with the work. When we finished the switching and put the train back together, ready to leave town, I started walking back to the hind end. The head end had the Yellow jack, so started to haul out, and the train got going pretty

* Took siding and reset the switch.

fast in no time. Remembering that there were all box cars on the rear end, I grabbed a handle* and went high while I could still make it.

Southbound out of Concord the yard tracks come into the main on a big, left-hand curve. Usually the head-end man looks back along the left side to see when the buggy comes out and watches for a highball motion from the rear.

I was making good time over the tops as we pulled out, but what I didn't know was that at Concord the yard switcher had cut in a string of empty hopper cars ahead of the buggy. I came to those dark, empty hoppers—and was trapped. By this time the train was going too fast for me to get off. I knew I could never hold out in the cold until we got to Manchester, our next stop. When I didn't show up in the buggy, the conductor would probably think I'd been left in Concord.

Luckily, I had a fusee in my pocket which lit on the first strike, and, luckily, the head-end man was looking back as usual. I waved the fusee like mad and right away heard the air go on. I unloaded as soon as the train slowed enough. I grabbed the buggy on the fly, threw the fusee away and swung a highball. Head end picked up and went along. The conductor, working on his bills, never knew what happened.

Another night, I was called for the flag on a Boston-Worcester run. While I was sweeping out the buggy and doing other chores a young man in a business suit and a felt hat climbed aboard, a bundle under his arm. I wondered what official this might be. He asked, "Is this BW-1?" I told him it was and asked who he was. He told me he was the head-end man. New man, first job. I guess my eyes bugged out so you could hang your hat on them. I asked if he knew we had steam on that job, and was he going to brake the head end in those clothes? He said he had his work clothes in the package and proceeded to get them out and put them on. I continued my work.

I was filling and lighting the markers when he came along and said:

"Pardon me, sir, where's the basement?"

I just didn't believe what I heard; I thought the guy was a nut. I asked him if he knew he was in a railroad car. He knew that, he said, but just had to go to the basement. I don't exactly recall how I got to the bottom of this, but it turned out that he was just recently from high school, where "the basement" was the little boy's room. When I told him what he had to do it was his turn to have *his* eyes bug out.

But he qualified as a flagman after a while, and one of his first flag jobs was on a night extra to Mechanicville, N.Y. Somewhere out west in the wilds of the Berkshire Hills they had a breakdown. The kid went back flagging while the conductor went up ahead with an armful of tools.

Eventually they were ready to go again. They called in the flag. The kid got on all right and stood on the rear buggy platform. The conductor headed for the

---

* Climb onto a ladder or grabirons to ride a car, usually when car is in motion.

rear end as they hauled along but, by the time the buggy came up to him, he figured that the train was going too fast for him to get aboard with all those tools. He heaved the tools onto the front platform but missed his grab to climb on by the rear steps.

"Don't go off and leave me!" he hollered at the kid standing on the platform. His intention was for the kid to pull the air and stop the train.

"I won't!" yelled the kid, and *he* unloaded.

Away went the train into the night, leaving those two standing by the track, looking at each other. I would like to have been a fly in a bush to hear what was said, and I'm glad it wasn't said to me.

I don't know how far they had to walk to arrive at a dispatcher's phone, but I can imagine the conversation, if any. Dispatcher stopped the next train that came along, and they got aboard. Later that night they caught up with their own train. The kid didn't stick with railroading—too bad, because he was as nice a guy as you could ask for, polite, a real gentleman, but he wouldn't have made a railroader if he lived to be a thousand. I heard later that he went into the dry-cleaning business and made good at it.

Although buggies had no wings, we sometimes "flew" them into the caboose tracks at Mystic.* This was a tricky stunt that required cooperation, technique and a bit of luck. We normally hauled in on a track called the "Fourth Iron," as I remember. After we left the main line at Winter Hill, or got well in off the Cut-off, we'd close the angle cock on the car just ahead of the buggy, using our bent iron rod. Then we'd bleed the air out of the buggy and, as we approached the hump, pull the pin on the head end of the buggy. Applying a little pinch of hand brake, we'd drop off the train. Once the train hauled away from us, we'd coast the buggy in, using the hand brake to keep far enough back so that the tower man could throw the iron into the buggy track after the last car of the train had cleared. Then we'd ride the buggy down to a soft hitch onto the others already on the buggy track.

That's the way the trick was *supposed* to work. If, however, we didn't pinch it down enough to open the gap between the buggy and the last car the tower man wouldn't throw the iron. On the other hand, if we squeezed it down too much we might stall the buggy on the hump itself—and have to listen to a lot of noise about it. I've had both these things happen to me. Also, I've had the misfortune to have the train suddenly stop and the buggy slam back into it before I could do anything. I got a good lecture that time on how to use a brake club. I nearly used it on the conductor the next time, when I stalled the buggy at the hump and had to listen to another lecture.

When one train goes by another, both headed in the same direction, the action is called "passing." When trains go by each other in opposite directions, the

* Mystic Junction, marshalling yards near North Station in Boston.

action is a "meet." To take care of these movements in single-track territory, the railroads have passing tracks, long sidings, with a switch at each end. The rule book states which train is "superior" to the other, and it's up to the "inferior" train to use the siding, when making the meet, unless instructed otherwise by a train order.

Quite often, when hauling down to a passing siding with the intention of heading into it, the engineer would slow down enough for the head brakeman to sprint ahead and open the switch, so that the train could go in without stopping. This helped the move, because a train with a roll on it was easy to keep rolling but, once stopped, it might be hard to start again.

This sprinting ahead to get the switch in front of a moving train was against the rules, yet we did it often. Working out of a diesel on the head end it was fairly easy because you got off at the cab end of the engine. On a steam engine, you had to be pretty spry to outrun the engine itself after dropping off at the gangway. I have done it both ways, and once with close to dire results. I stepped off the engine when it was going a mite faster than I could run. The result was a bruising cartwheel by me, down the bank into the bushes—the last time I ever pulled *that* stunt.

I remember another instance of taking a siding that way, on the fly. We were to haul in for a meet with a passenger train; I dropped off and scooted for the switch. It was dark. I had some trouble with the switch lock so that by the time I was through fumbling and ready to throw the switch the headlight of the engine was practically over my head. I grabbed the switch handle, but didn't dare to move it for fear I'd put the engine on the ground. The train headed straight down the main line.

It took the engineer a few seconds to realize where he was going. He was some three or four car lengths beyond the switch before applying the air. Now he had to shove back until he cleared the switch, so I could throw it. We had a heavy train, on a grade, and he couldn't move it at first. After taking slack three or four times he finally managed to get us back behind the switch. But now the passenger train was due, and the fireman had to go out the main line and flag it. I wasn't exactly popular for the rest of the job.

Once, on symbol freight JB-490, we had a night meet at Penacook with "three-and-a-quarter," train No. 325. It was one of those nights when the low spots and river valleys were full of fog. Situated low in the Merrimac River valley, Penacook was blanketed solid.

I had the flag on the job and dropped off, when we hauled in, to line the switch behind us. The buggy hadn't gone three car lengths from me when it was completely out of sight in the fog. But I could hear them hauling down until, after what seemed to me a long time, I heard the slack run in. All was quiet. I followed down the passing track to the rear end of the train. Nothing to do now but wait for 325.

The time for the passenger train to arrive came, and went. Then we heard No. 325 blow two whistles. There was steam on 325, a 3700, as I recall, and we had a diesel. Now what could three-and-a-quarter be whistling for? Conductor and I were on the rear platform, listening. Next thing we heard was our diesel whistle twice. Then, after a short space of time, 325 whistled out a flag and our diesel sounded three blasts, the signal to back up. Soon the slack ran in, and we shoved back a few car lengths. Again all was quiet.

We were pretty confused there on the rear end, so the conductor said he'd hike up ahead to see what was going on and would stay at the head end to get the main-line switch when we pulled out. I was to hold our train with the air if, in the fog, it looked as though he couldn't grab the buggy and would be left behind. Then No. 325 called in their flag and, after a while, went by and away into the fog toward the north. As we sat still, time dragging on, I listened to them whistling on toward Franklin.

Now behind us somewhere was the milk train. They had been making up in White River as we pulled out of there, and could be expected to meet 325 at Franklin. But, just how close were they? I sat there thinking that if they were to come along while we were pulling out of the siding, I'd have to stick a fusee out on the main line in front of them or, if we stayed in the clear, I'd have to turn our markers to show green to the rear. Then I began to hear a diesel horn from behind us there in the night.

As the sound came closer I could estimate the speed at which they were coming. Also, I supposed that our head end had not opened the main-line switch; therefore I turned the markers. Pretty soon the milk train came flying out of the fog and on by with a clatter. Only then did we move.

Let's go back to what was happening at the head end while we were waiting for No. 325 to meet us. We had hauled down the passing track to what the engineer *thought* was the clearance point. Nevertheless, due to the bad visibility because of the soupy fog, he'd gone by it just far enough to foul the main line by a hair. This put him across the insulated track joint, so that the opposing signals changed to a restrictive indication. This was fortunate because, when 325 came along, they had to make a "know nothing" stop, whistle twice and come along at restricted speed. Then, as they appeared out of the fog, our engineer gave them two whistles to come on, never dreaming that we weren't wholly in the clear. Before anything could be done to prevent it, they sideswiped us—just barely. Of course, they stopped to assess damage and our engineer shoved back, sounding the prescribed three blasts. There was no great harm done—a few grabirons torn off the diesel and some gouges on 325's steam engine—but it caused a few anxious moments and, yes, the inevitable investigation.

Brakemen would constantly watch the cars on curves . . .

 # Freight Train Troubles

A QUICK LOOK AT A FREIGHT CAR AND ONE WOULDN'T THINK THERE'S MUCH CAN GO wrong. You see a body on top of a pair of four-wheel trucks, and a coupler and a hose sticking out at each end under the car floor. Simple, you say, just hook up and highball. Let's look a little closer first.

In my day there were mostly box cars, which they loaded with things that had to be protected from the weather. Next in number were the hopper cars which they loaded with coal, crushed stone or any bulk load that could dump out through trap doors in the bottom. Heavyweight stuff from logs to machinery

47

Hard to say what gave us the most trouble on freight runs, broken knuckles, stuck pins, pulled drawbars, but perhaps it was the running gear instead, especially the journal boxes on the trucks.

rode on a flat car, or "gon"—gondola, that is—which is just a flat car with sides so it can also handle material like sand, ore, or scrap metal. Today they put a lot of specialized types into a train, but my memory is that tank cars and "reefers"—refrigerator cars—were mostly what we handled in the way of special purpose cars. No matter how a car looks on top, underneath they hang a lot of tricky hardware which is about the same no matter what kind of car it is.

The couplers were automatic, so called. This meant we didn't have to go between to line things up when two cars came together, but we'd have to get in there to join up the hoses and make sure there was a good hitch. The couplers were metal castings at the end of a shaft, or drawbar, the "knuckle" part, like a handclasp, pivoting to release or make the hitch. A pin dropped into place, after coupling, to keep the knuckle from releasing and losing the hitch. The pin was attached by a chain or rod to a release rod. This extended across the bottom of the end of the car and was bent at the ends so that we could turn the rod up, pulling the pin and uncoupling the car. The hose couplings would come apart by themselves. Hard to say what gave us the most trouble on freight runs, broken knuckles, stuck pins, pulled drawbars, but perhaps it was the running gear instead, especially the journal boxes on the trucks, which housed the bearings for the wheel axles, and could raise cain in the form of hot boxes.

Hot boxes were constantly a problem on freight trains. We were always on the lookout for them. A journal could run hot from lack of oil, or from a "waste grab" or from the entry of some foreign matter under the lids. The lack of oil might be caused by a leaky journal, a fault that should have been found beforehand by the car knockers back at the terminal. A waste grab was a condition where a little shred of cotton waste from the bottom of the journal wormed up under the brass bearing. This would make a box run hot in no time!

Whenever we saw that our train had a heavy car of sand, or a reefer with its ice bunker drip chutes missing, we could expect hot boxes. Cars hauling sand or like material were very heavy, and one or more of the car's eight journals could heat up fast on long through-freight runs. The telltale dribble of white brine on the truck frame of a refrigerator car spelled trouble, because the brine would get into a journal, and we'd have a hot one, sure enough.

Brakemen on both ends of any fast freight constantly would watch the cars on curves, "looking 'em over" for signs of smoke or flame. Either one meant stop the train and trudge down to the hot one, try to cool it off enough to haul slowly to the next siding and set the car off. Real "flamers" under wooden box cars or tank cars of gasoline were dangerous.

Many times a single hot box delayed us an hour or more. On trains of eighty-five to ninety cars, with a hot one in the middle, it took considerable time just getting to the car with the trouble. Another ten or fifteen minutes would be spent putting out the fire and cooling off the journal. Then the long hike back to the head or rear end took another five or ten minutes. Hauling along to the nearest siding at about ten miles an hour for perhaps four or five miles, then setting off the car, was a thirty or forty minute job at best. It seems to me now that it was usually nighttime, the siding would be short and dark and the train on a curve; so that the whole crew had to spread out along the car tops passing motions with fusees.

Although probably the most numerous, hot boxes were not our only troubles. Another difficulty which could give us considerable grief was a break-in-two, a parting of the train. Coming unhitched like this was, naturally, accompanied by an emergency brake application. You'll see.

Break-in-twos could be caused by weak or defective knuckles, or drawbars, or rough handling, or trying to start a train with the rear end tied down by the brakes—or too much gusto on the head end of a long train with a lot of slack.

Sometimes only a knuckle would let go, sometimes just a pin broke. But sometimes the whole drawbar broke off, or the entire draft-gear rigging pulled out. Knuckles were fairly easy to replace; we carried spares in the buggy, usually, but we might have to steal one off the nose of the engine. This, of course, meant lugging a piece of heavy iron perhaps thirty-five or more car lengths. Still, that's easy compared to the trouble you have with a busted drawbar.

A broken drawbar usually rolled under the train until the train came to a stop. In doing so it could, if your luck was out, rip off the brake rigging of the cars it went under. A dropped drawbar could roll any old which way, like a log or end over end, or catch on the ties and bump along, as unpredictable as the bounce of a football. I've seen one trip on a tie, up end and rip open the hopper of a hopper car of coal, dumping the load on the track. They've been known to derail the whole works, too. In fact, whatever the cause, the emergency application of brakes as a result of a break-in-two could cause derailments of major proportions—wrecks, as a matter of fact.

If we couldn't put things back together with a new knuckle or pin, the only thing left to do was get rid of the crippled car. First, we had to drag all the broken parts out from under the train—drawbars, draft gear, release rods and what not. This stuff had to be rolled down the bank away from the track. Also it paid to look the cars over, underneath, to see what else might have been knocked loose and left hanging. What we had to do depended a lot on where the break was located in a train and on which end of a car the damage was done.

Take it that a broken drawbar had been on the rear end of a car in the forward section of a train. We would haul the cars on the engine, including the cripple, to the nearest side track, leaving the hind end of the train where it was. After getting rid of the cripple we'd shove back, pick up the rest of the train and go along. (Except that if the cripple was a car of perishables we'd have to back the put-together train into the siding and tie the cripple on behind the buggy, then move along.)

Now, if the break was on the head end of the car, we'd have to chain the cripple to the car ahead of it. Some stunt, especially in a snowstorm and having to lug all that heavy chain fifty car-lengths, say, from the caboose. Then we'd pull the pin *behind* the cripple, take head-end cars and cripple to siding, *un*chain and go back to pick up the rest of the train.

Such a break way back in the train—we called it "getting one on the foolish end"—meant we'd have to take all the cars ahead of it to a siding that would hold them. Go back to the cripple with engine. Chain it to engine, pull pin behind cripple, take it to some other siding, leave it, pick up the head-end cars, return to hind end, couple up and go along. We'd be lucky in this situation, in double-track territory, when there was a crossover handy. Traffic permitting, we could just back the head-end cars across the road, then proceed to get rid of the cripple as above.

In bad weather, with poor visibility, a drawbar break in a long train (whether on the foolish end or not) was all the trouble one could ask for.

Though almost everyone knows that trains have air brakes, not everybody knows how they work. Without going into all the details of Mr. Westinghouse's invention, let me just say that the brakes are held released—meaning "off"—by the balance of pressure between each car's brake cylinder reservoir and the train line. To "put on" brakes, the engineer reduces the train-line pressure by a valve provided in the cab and the resulting *un*balance causes the brakes to be applied. The force with which they are applied depends on *how much* reduction in the train line. On a long train the reduction is felt at the head end first, so that the brakes go on progressively, front to rear. The lag between the braking at the head end and the rear end is not much, but it's enough so that the slack has a tendency to bunch.

Now and then we'd get what was called a "kicker," a car with a defective valve on its brake cylinder slung underneath. When the train-line reduction called for a normal service application of brakes the kicker's valve would open wide, dumping all the air out of the train line under that car, putting the brakes into emergency application. Call it "going into the big hole." This would trigger the same action in every car from the kicker forward and rearward. When this happens, the slack between the kicker and the head end doesn't bunch. It stretches.

Somewhere between the kicker and the head end there may be a weak draw-bar, and away it goes! It may be just your luck to have it on the foolish end. Now the break-in-two is obvious—provided the train wasn't derailed by the emergency stop—so we get rid of the cripple as described. However, that freaky valve is not something visible to the train crew. After putting their train back together they still have this culprit, and the brakes can go emergency again the first time the engineer applies the air.

When the train-line pressure is dumped, the brakes get clamped on tight. The only way to get started again is to charge the whole train line, to keep on pumping until all brakes are pumped off. On long trains, even a diesel took quite a while to accomplish this and a steam engine took still longer. I have seen trains that had so many leaky valves that it was all the pump could do to get the brakes released.

Other troubles: We'd sometimes have flat wheels banging and brake rigging dragging. A dragging brake rigging might not do worse than cut up the ties until, perhaps, part of it caught on a switch rod. This would pull the switch open and then, of course, things piled sky high! Because of this risk, when we spotted a dragging brake rigging, we'd crawl under, disconnect it and get rid of it. Picture lying on your back some night under a dripping hide car,* say, disconnecting a brake rigging by the light of a lantern.

Coming inward on JB-490 one night, we picked up Boston cars as usual at Lowell. As we came around the curve by Billerica Shop I looked back on the engineer's side to see how things were. Back there among our Lowell pickups I saw fire flying, not the hot-box type of flame, but sparks caused by something dragging, or scraping a wheel, or the rail. We stopped, but so did the sparks. I went back for a look, but could find nothing wrong. At Silver Lake I saw sparks again, and pretty well located where they were. We hauled down to Wilmington and stopped. This time I found it. A loose brake shoe was slapping against a wheel, throwing a pinwheel of sparks every time it hit. No real damage done; we went right on into Boston. But those sparks were something spectacular!

I propose to the reader this situation: You are the conductor of a crew of three on an eighty-five car freight. It's a cold, rainy night, but you're making good time. Somewhere around the middle of the train you have a car throwing fire such as I've described. Yet it can't be seen from either end of the train. The weather is just too thick.†

As you go flying through a grade crossing the crossing tender sees it—all too well—and gives the boys on the rear end a "washout." A washout is a stop motion given with a certain amount of urgency that calls for action, so that the boys on the buggy go after the air with a little too much gusto. And a kicker toward the rear dumps the air into the big hole, tying the hind end down tight while the engine still hauls on at forty miles an hour.

Near the head end is an old box car that has been running around for years. The strain on the old crate is too great, so—whango—out goes a drawbar, on the foolish end. Because the air has gone into emergency for reasons unknown to the head end and the train is in double-track territory, the head brakeman goes up flagging the other main line as per rule 102.** Assume you're the conductor, and you start slogging ahead through the rain. Hind-end flagman goes back to protect the rear, so he's of no use any more.

There's been no derailment—this time—so you have to go way up to the head end to have them call in the head brakeman. You and he chain up the cripple

---

* Usually an old wooden box car which, once it was used for hides, couldn't be used for anything else and was marked "Hides Only" on the outside. Though they were not reefers, they dripped whatever it is that drips out of hides.

† B&M twists around so, there are few places where the middle of an eighty-five car train can be seen from either end in any weather.

** Rule 102. When a train is disabled or stopped suddenly by an emergency application of the air brakes, or other causes, adjacent tracks as well as tracks of other railroads that are liable to be obstructed must at once be protected until it is ascertained they are safe and clear for the movement of trains.

and haul down four or five miles to back it off into a siding. Then you shove back through the gloom to pick up the rest of the train. You still don't know why the crossing tender gave you the washout. You can find nothing wrong. Neither can you find the kicker. There's only yourself and the head-end man to do the work, and you didn't have him until he was called back from flagging. . . .

Did I hear someone recently suggest that railroads could save money by having only an engineer and a conductor on those trains?

On another night we were picking up cars in Lowell when we heard the "kaBUNK, kaBUNK" sound of a flat wheel among the pickups. We looked 'em over and found a wheel with a piece the size of one's hand gone out of the tread. We switched the car out and left it in Lowell. It probably couldn't have made it to Boston before the wheel broke, and the whole outfit landed in someone's back yard.

Troubles? Yes, we had a few.

Hump yard at "Mystic"

7

"Two In, Two Out, Shove In and Set"

FREIGHT SERVICE IS A LITTLE DIFFERENT NOW FROM WHAT IT WAS IN THOSE DAYS. But then there were the symbol freights BU-3, Boston to White River Junction, Vermont, daytimes, and BU-1, Boston to White River Junction nights, also UB-2 and JB-490, both night jobs, White River to Boston. There was a BW-1, Boston to Worcester, turn on a wheel and back to Boston as WB-2. BP-5 and PB-4 ran Boston to Portland and return over the Portland Division. We'll take a ride on BP-5 later on in this book. Meantime, other symbol freights I remember were a "WL" job between Worcester and Lawrence and the "CW" job between Concord and Worcester. There were other jobs I seldom covered, but saw and heard much about: Boston-Mechanicville—we called it "Mickeyville"—in New York, Portland-Mickeyville, Boston-Rotterdam Junction (N.Y.), Portland-Worcester and Boston-Bellows Falls, Vermont. These last were called "BX" jobs and saw the final use of the 2900 series of Santa Fe-type engines, the mudsuckers.

These Symbol Freights were also referred to as "high wheel" jobs. They were really transfer operations, taking whole trains from one interchange point to another, a "bridge operation," so called. For example, RM-1 ran from Rigby, our connection with the Maine Central, to Mechanicville, where we connected with the Delaware & Hudson. Eastbound, Mechanicville to Boston, the train symbol was MB-2.

I used to be called for numerous high wheel extra trains, such as the "potato extras" during potato season in Maine. We would have a train of empties out of Boston, or Worcester, to Portland, and return with full tonnage, usually *all* potatoes. Sometimes, if business warranted, we'd have merchandise "Deerfield extras," Boston to East Deerfield and return, hauling full tonnage each way. Yet I recall one extra, Concord to East Deerfield, when we went out with an empty coal car and the buggy hauled by a four-unit diesel. The engine was longer than the train! However, coming back, we had all the cars we could wiggle and had to have a pusher behind the buggy from East Deerfield to Gardner.

Boston cars off these freights were for the most part intended for consignees served by local freights working out of Boston in all directions. The locals were the peddlers, door-to-door, so to speak.

Nearly all our locals originated in Boston, more commonly known as Mystic Junction, or just plain "Mystic." These locals were usually day jobs starting out of Mystic in the morning. They would be made up in "station order" whenever possible so that the head cars could be left off at the first place arrived at, the next ones at the second place, and so on. This didn't always work out, but the yardmaster tried to do it that way.

At the Mystic yard office the conductor would receive a bundle of waybills, all in station order, the top bill for the head car, etc. He'd also probably get a "stripper," a long card form on which the cars were listed in order, giving the car number, its reporting marks (SF, MEC, IC, NYC, etc.) and the consignee. If all we had to do was peddle cars and make no pickups, things would be simple. Just deal 'em off the top of the deck. As soon as we started picking up loads or empties, things would get complicated and the chess game commenced. This meant that the conductor would have to think out and give us specific moves to be made at various sidings. For instance, if we had picked up two empties on the head end (or "head pin," as we'd also say) and the next two cars were to go into a siding, the conductor's call might be: "Cut behind four. Put two in, two out, shove in and set."

This directs us to pull the pin behind the fourth head car, kick the two hind ones into the siding, kick the two head ones back onto the train and then, with the engine, shove the two cars for the siding back in to be set at a platform, door or other unloading spot.

At such places as North Somerville, West Medford, Wilmington, Woburn and like towns, where there was a district agent, he would give the conductor further instructions as to which consignees had cars coming out and where the consignees wanted cars set. Then we'd have to do local switching, in which process we'd try to put any Boston-bound cars next to the buggy. All our movements had to be done while keeping out of the way of First Class trains. We were supposed to be in the clear at the time any First Class train was due to leave the next station behind us. If we were working the main line there were times when we couldn't get much done. Another requirement was not to arrive at a siding, to get in the clear, with more cars than the siding would hold.

I did see this happen a few times on the West Medford job, which usually had a lot of work at the Container Corporation and Simmons Mattress plants just south of West Medford. The normal move was to switch out the Container and Simmons cars at West Medford, getting them in the proper order. Then we'd leave the buggy and the balance of our train in the clear and take the switched-out cars down to the Container, leaving the flagman at West Medford so we could shove back there under flag protection when we were through at the Container and Simmons. But there'd be times when a conductor would think he could get the whole train into the clear at the Container, only to find that it wouldn't all fit there. Now what?

Often this would be about the time of a southbound passenger train, and there's some of our train hanging out on the main line. We'd have to leave the flagman at the Container switch and take everything that wouldn't fit all the way to North Somerville before getting into the clear. After the passenger train went, we'd shove back up the southbound main, under flag protection, and resume our work at the Container. What a waste of time—when the trainmaster learned about it he usually had a few things to say to the conductor!

The crew of a local freight consisted of conductor, head brakeman and a flagman with, of course, an engineer and fireman on the engine. However, in double-track territory it was necessary for some jobs to "cross the road" to the other main line to switch tracks on that side. The move had to be done under flag protection on both main lines. Jobs involving this move carried a fourth man called the "middle man" or "swing man." His chief purpose was to carry out the crossover move while the head-end man flagged the other main line. He assisted in other moves as well, sometimes riding the engine, sometimes the buggy, hence the name "swing man."

The usual way into a siding was through a "trailing point" switch; the engine could shove cars into the siding on a *back up* move. But there were some places where the siding would have a "facing point" switch. This meant that the engine had to nose in, and we'd have to get cars from behind onto the nose of the engine so that they could be *pushed* in. It was easy if there was a passing siding handy for a run-around; if not, we had to pull a flying switch, known on the B&M as "flying 'em by." This should be done by three men, though it can be handled in a pinch by two. One man is stationed at the switch, one man rides the car to set up a hand brake and somebody has to pull the pin behind the engine. When things are all set, the engineer gets a roll on the car in the direction of the switch. He then shuts off a little to give us some slack, and we pull the head pin. Then he works steam down the main line to outrun the car. Soon as the engine clears the switch, the switch is thrown, and the car comes rolling along and turns into the siding. The engine comes back, noses into the siding and sets the car.

Sounds simple, but I've seen some hairy moves resulting in a car slamming through the bunter* at the end of the siding, or stopping too short of the clearance point. In the latter case, the car would have to be "staked out" of the siding and the move tried again. The stake, or pole, was a husky timber hung on the side of the engine tender. It had to be positioned between the poling socket of the tender and a like socket on the end sill of the car. With this pole the car was given a shove out through the switch. Again, it sounds simple, but, if there was a slip-up, you'd be treated to the sight of a flying pole and a jouncing car. Quite

---

* Bumper, but on the B&M I never heard it as anything but "bunter."

something to behold—and an easy way for somebody to get hurt.

When we arrived at a town or yard, or other place where there was considerable switching to do, we usually "kicked cars" up various sidings and tracks in order to rearrange our train. To kick a car was to give it a smart shove with the engine, pull the pin and let it go. Before the move we'd have to bleed the air. Every car had a "bleed rod" sticking out from under it, which we could pull and thus release the air from the brake reservoir. The car was then free to roll. Woburn yard was one location where a lot of car kicking took place. The yard tracks were on a slight grade, so that someone had to catch all the cars and trig them with sticks of wood under a wheel to keep them from rolling back. Things could get pretty lively up there, with one man throwing switches, another pulling pins and another running around trigging cars.

After the switching was done, and the train put back together, the air line had to be hooked up between each car and all angle cocks opened. It required a certain technique to connect those stiff hoses. I've seen a green man struggle with them and work his life out until someone showed him how to do it. The technique was to grasp the nearest, or right-hand, hose and, with a quick flip, double it back on itself. Then grab the other hose, bring it up and drop the connections together. That sounds simple, too, but it took practice.

Figuring out all these moves required no small skill if they were to be done in the shortest time and the least amount of motion. A new man could fool around for half an hour or more while an experienced man would have all the cars set and ready to leave town before you knew it.

One other thing that took some thought was the arrangement of cars for a consignee with two tracks alongside one platform, where cars on the outside

The locals used steam engines of all types . . .

track would have to be loaded or unloaded *through* the cars on the platform track. When the cars were set the car doors had to line up. Now some cars were 40-footers and some were 50-footers, so a conductor would have to figure his work in order to set both tracks right. The Container Corporation was just such a place; moreover, it was necessary to handle the cars here very carefully because some of them would be partially unloaded. In these cars the remaining contents would not be shored up, so that rough treatment could dump the whole works over inside a car.

As I mentioned in the chapter on "Head End," the locals used steam engines of all types, 0–6–0's, 0–8–0's, Moguls, K-8's. These engines all came from the main terminal at Mystic, and are all gone now, having been replaced by diesels.

Some Local Freights

All three B&M divisions ran locals out of Mystic, though I was most familiar with those of the New Hampshire Division, on which we had five trains going every day except Sunday. These jobs had numbers, but we had names for them that we always used instead, even the crew dispatcher when calling crews. There was the Woburn job, the West Medford job, the Marlboro job, the Bedford job—known as the "BB"—and the Wilmington job we referred to as "the Willie."

First out in the morning was the Woburn local up the New Hampshire Division main line, setting off cars at West Medford Middle to be picked up by the West Medford local. It then went along to Winchester, and to Woburn via the Woburn Loop. They switched Woburn yard, keeping clear of No. 3320, a train hauled by one of the remaining 3200 Class 4–4–2 Atlantics that came out of

One of the remaining 3200 Class 4–4–2 Atlantics . . .

Boston as a deadhead train, turned at Woburn and left there at 11:00 A.M. for Boston as a commuter train. The Woburn freight local then went back down the Loop to do local switching. At Winchester they crossed the road and backed up to Beggs & Cobb tannery. Then they went back to Winchester and up the main line to Swanton Street yard, where they switched out the Winchester Brick and Rock track. From Swanton Street they went back to Boston.

The Wilmington local went out the New Hampshire Division, setting off cars at North Somerville, for the West Medford local. Occasionally the Willie would be called upon to switch the Rouse Vinegar works at Somerville Junction, but after the North Somerville chore they'd go north to do the necessary work at Banter Coal. Then up to Winchester, where they were crossed over and went along to Winchester Highlands. From here they backed down into Swanton Street yard, did the switching across the road at the J. O. Witten works, and switched out their Stoneham cars, moving up the main line to Montvale, and the Stoneham Branch. At Farm Hill they'd work the Hercules Powder Co. siding, then local switching at Stoneham itself. Coming back down the branch, there was work to do at Atlantic Gelatin. They'd left the Gelatin cars at the passing track, on the way up.

Back now to Montvale, to Winchester Highlands and Swanton Street yard (their Boston cars from the branch had been left here). Here they picked up their Wilmington cars and went north, on the main line, to South Wilmington, where they switched out the Consolidated Chemical and General Foods plants. Go along north again through North Woburn Junction to Wilmington, where they hauled into the Wilmington Junction Branch to turn around, putting the engine over the table at the engine house and taking water. After putting the train together there was local switching to be done, then to head south again when they "got a run" from the dispatcher. At South Wilmington they'd have to switch the International Fertilizer plant before moving on south once more into Walnut Hill. Very little work there, and so on back to Winchester Highlands, pull in and down to Swanton Street yard. Here they would pick up their Boston cars and, when traffic permitted, go into Boston.

The West Medford local left Mystic with its 0–8–0 600 Class engine running backwards. They did some switching at North Somerville on the northbound side and then went to West Medford, where they did considerable switching with the cars the Woburn job had set off on the middle track, most of them for the Container Corporation and Simmons. After doing the work at the Container, as described earlier, they went back to North Somerville and did local switching for the rest of the day. Finally, they'd go into Mystic, stopping at Agar's on the Freight Cut-off at Somerville Junction to set up the Agar cars at the platform.

Though it was covered by New Hampshire Division crews in my time, the Marlboro job actually operated over the old Central Massachusetts branch as far out as Hudson and Marlboro. The BB local went from Boston to West Cambridge on the Fitchburg Division, but from there up the Lexington Branch through Arlington and Lexington to Bedford, doing the work at Hanscomb Air Base and, if needed, at Concord, Massachusetts. Afterward, it proceeded on up through Billerica to the main line at North Billerica, switching the back side of Billerica Shop if necessary, then on up the main line to Lowell. Turning on the New Haven wye at Lowell, the BB came back to the Lowell south yard where they picked up both Billerica Shop cars and Boston cars. Returning via the main line, they'd set off and pick up at Billerica Shop, then get back to Boston.

The Fitchburg Division regularly had B9, B10, the Ayer local, also a Watertown local, a Waltham local and the West Cambridge job.

On Portland Division, there were two "East Route" jobs from Boston to Salem, doing the local work between. One was called the "Morning Glory" and the other, the "Camel." Don't ask me how they got the names. While the Morning Glory took care of the Salem work, the Camel poked along to as far as Newburyport or even Portsmouth, working sidings and yards beyond Salem. The "Chelsea Goat" was another local freight on the East Route, spending all day around Chelsea and Revere, and the Saugus local traveled the East Route as far as Everett Junction—the scene of a spectacular rear-end collision in 1871 on the then Eastern Railroad—and they did all the switching on the Saugus Branch as far as West Lynn.

Portland Division had a West Route, too, as the map shows, on which the Medford local did the Medford Branch work before going up to spend the rest of the day at Oak Grove in Malden. One other local I remember was the Reading local, also known as the "High Car" for a very good reason. At Salem there was a tunnel through which trains ducked under some streets right after leaving the station to go on to Beverly. Just fine for trains with cars of standard height, but cars exceeding the vertical clearances in that tunnel had to be routed around it. Any of these eastbound out of Boston to destinations beyond Salem got hung onto the Reading local, which went via Lynnfield and Peabody to Salem's North River yard. So the Reading job was also called the "High Car" in spite of the fact that this local's job was in main-line territory, Oak Grove, Wakefield and Reading, even as far north as North Wilmington.

Considering all these locals weaving in and out of side tracks and branch lines and on to main lines, as well as the many First Class trains we had in the '40s, it becomes quite evident that General Rule A was important to the safe operation of trains. General Rule A reads, in part:

> "Employees whose duties are in any way affected by the timetable
> must have a copy of the current timetable with them while on duty."

Not only did we have a copy but we had to know how to read it. It helped, too, if our many passengers knew how to read the public timetable. Many did know how, but some read it wrong, as in the following instance:

Where the "High Car" couldn't go

A friend of mine tells me about one night he was coming up from New York to Greenfield. He caught a train out of Grand Central to Springfield, where he had to transfer to a Connecticut River line B&M train that terminated at Northampton, even though he had a ticket through to Greenfield.

Conductor came through and punched the ticket. Some minutes later he was back, asking my friend:

"Do you have someone meeting you at Northampton, who will drive you to Greenfield?"

My friend said that, yes, that was his situation.

"Would you," then asked the conductor, "be willing to take another passenger with you?"

My friend said he'd be delighted to help a fellow traveler in need. Indeed, the idea of having to get off at Northampton, unless one happened to live there, or have a date with a Smith College lovely, was not one hundred per-cent appealing. In his opinion, that is.

"This passenger," continued the conductor, "who is riding in the car just back of this one, will be grateful. He is on his way from Washington to his place in Chester, Vermont, there to spend a relaxing weekend. He confesses that he read the timetable wrong, resulting in the impression that this train goes through to Greenfield, where there will be an auto to take him on to Chester."

My friend observed that even in this year of our Lord, 1952, when the Boston & Maine was being complimented on the design and clear printing of its timetables, one could occasionally slip up, with, who knows, what consequences.

"For your information," added the conductor, "this passenger's name is French, Edward French. He is the President of the Boston & Maine Railroad."

The B&M had sixteen of these 2-8-4 Berkshires.

Night Freight

To FURTHER THESE RECOLLECTIONS, LET'S TAKE A TRIP TO RIGBY YARD, PORTLAND, Maine, on BP-5. Let's assume that you, the reader, are along as a working "observer"; you might as well be swing man on this job. We're for the head end, called for duty at 7:30, leaving time, 8:00 P.M. Our train is stretched out through Yard 9 at Mystic Junction, so the first thing is a long walk down to where we should be. It is summer time, and it is hot.

All these trains are looked over before leaving Boston, to spot and correct such things as hand brakes tightened up, swinging doors on refrigerator cars, retainer valves on the brake cylinders turned down as they should be, or anything that looks defective. You go down one side, I'll go down the other. The late sun is burning down into the "alleys" between the tracks, just sizzling. Perhaps we'll have cooler weather down Portland way.

When we arrive at the head end we see that the engine has not yet come on but has gone down past Tower "C" toward Yard 21. It will soon come back. The car knocker is waiting here, and the conductor. Here comes the engine backing through the switches, the fireman looking back on the inside of the curves, and calling signals.

The engine is No. 4017, a big 2–8–4 Berkshire type with low drivers, quite capable for the job. She clumps back as we motion her down slowly until, with a clash, she "clasps hands" with BP-5. The engineer eases her forward to take the slack and make sure the hitch is made. The car knocker hooks up the hose and the 4017 starts pumping air to charge the train line. The conductor has the dope on the night's work; we climb into the cab with him and learn what we have to do.

The job has eighty-seven cars tonight, counting the buggy. On the head end are fourteen cars for Lawrence, then eleven Haverhills. Eight empty gondolas for Rockingham come next, followed by six Biddefords, twenty-five Dovers and, on the hind end, twenty-two for Rigby. Those Biddeford cars out of place ahead of the Dovers must mean that we are going to pick cars up in Dover tonight. The conductor hands us a stripper with all this dope, giving us the name and number of the last car of each cut we'll have to make.

The conductor slides down and lights out for the hind end. As soon as we have train-line pressure showing on the gage, the engineer sets the brakes with a roar of escaping air and a hefty blast from the 4017's whistle. One car knocker starts back along the train, inspecting brakes; another starts working forward from the buggy. We stand in the left gangway looking along the train to watch for the car knockers' signal to release brakes. The fireman has the stoker grumbling away under the cab deck, and the blower is roaring up the short, stubby stack. A column of smoke mounts into the hot evening air.

In a few minutes we see a car knocker giving the release motion from the top of a car midway along the train. We tell the engineer, "OK on the brakes. Let 'em off." Another exhaust of air from the brake stand, and two long whistles. The car knocker disappears, but he will come toward the head end. A passenger train, No. 169, moves out past Tower "C." We'll be following that train but probably won't see anything of them. Car knocker arrives alongside.

"Eighty-seven cars all working!" he shouts.

"OK. Gone from here!" shouts the engineer, and punctuates his reply with two short blasts of 4017's whistle. A bell starts clanging up forward and 4017 starts to take out the slack.

We step up to our seat behind the fireman and start looking sharp for switches and signals. On the left-hand curve out of the yard the engineer can't see around the boiler barrel, so can't tell what he's coming to until 4017's pilot is right on top of it. Right at this moment we're his eyes. Way ahead down the track the first switch, a Tower "C" operated one, looks wrong. "Bad iron!" we call. The engineer shuts off a little and 4017 yelps out four short blasts, urging Tower "C" to straighten things out. Immediately the pot signal whirls around. "OK on the iron!" we shout, and the throttle is "latched out" again.

We're through the switch and on the straight yard lead track taking us under the bridges at Sullivan Square. This yard lead runs all the way out to Wellington over Draw 8 on the Mystic River bridge. On this track, called the "Medford Track," we must run at restricted speed. Since it's almost two miles out to the crossover to the main line at Wellington we have a little time to look at our surroundings.

No. 4017 is one of the T-1a Class of engines built by Lima in 1928. The B&M had sixteen of these 2–8–4 Berkshires. They had 63″ drivers, 28 × 30″ cylinders, 240 pounds steam pressure and were good freight haulers, even better, as some thought, than the later and bigger 4100's. From our perch behind the fireman we glance around the cab. Just ahead of us the fireman sits, manipulating valves which operate the stoker, one to control the direction and speed of the stoker worm, others to control steam jets for distributing coal to desired spots in the firebox. He also has valves for the blower and for feedwater. These engines have a feedwater pump in addition to the injector. When everything is running right, the water level in the boiler is easy to control. We can see the level in the gage glasses on the water columns, illuminated by little hooded lights, one on each side of the boiler butt.

On top of the boiler butt is the steam gage, also illuminated by a hooded light. Lower down, on a shelf on the boiler backhead, is a place to put kerosene torches and long-necked oil cans. Below this is the firebox split door, operated by compressed air. The panels of the door slide sideways to open and shut.

On the engineer's side, there's a horizontally mounted throttle quadrant and the hand-wheel operated power reverse gear (which replaced the old Johnson Bar manual rig). Under the engineer's hand is the brake stand with its lever operating the valve that controls the train line, and a smaller one for the engine brakes, the "joker," as it is also called. Valves for the lubricator, bell ringer, whistle, sander, feedwater pump and booster* decorate the boiler butt. Overhead are switches for the classification lamps (out front on the smokebox) and back-up light (on the rear of the tender), and the switch for the headlight with "bright" or "dim" positions.

Behind us, across the "apron" between engine and tender—or "tank," which is the railroad man's usual name for it—loom the coal gates, which hold back a coal pile as high as the cab roof, or we'd have it right here in the cab. We'll eat into this pile generously before Rigby Yard is reached. The coal gates are closed now, but before the night is over we will have pulled a few slides from over the stoker pit, those coal gates will be open and we can walk right into the coal pile between the "tank legs" flanking the gates. The space between the tank legs and the cab back is where we get on and off the engine, the gangways. On top of the tank leg on the right-hand side is the icebox and water jug. The opposite tank leg has a compartment where repose two oil lanterns and other flagging equipment for use whenever we have to flag the main ahead of the train.

During all this time we've been looking things over, BP-5 has been moving out across the Mystic River. As we approach the far end of the Medford Track we're looking for the jack at the crossover. It has been showing Red, but just now changes to Yellow. The engineer calls, "Yellow eye!" The fireman confirms. He calls, "Yellow!" and widens on the blower and the stoker. It will be practically all uphill for seven miles, from here to Greenwood. With eighty-seven cars on behind, the 4017 will need steam. The fact that it's a hot summer night won't help 4017 one bit; coal and lots of draft is what she needs. The sun is dropping, red, toward the hazy western horizon. We have the heat of the firebox on top of the heat of the day.

No. 4017 twists through the crossover, taking BP-5 onto the outward, or eastbound, main. We look back on our side, watching the cars as they snake through. At last the hind end appears. As it swings across we call, "Green eye on the buggy!" signifying the hind end is through the crossovers. The engineer latches open the throttle. No. 4017 blasts off for Rigby Yard—111 miles away.

As we stamp by the numerous grade-crossing flashers at Wellington, and over the interlocking switches for the Medford Branch, the train is nosing into the

---

* The 4017's booster was on her rear truck.

grade up which the line climbs out of the Mystic River valley. Though it levels off a bit, from Oak Grove to Wyoming, it's on this grade that the 4017 settles down to moving her tonnage. The Malden gas works lie on our right, the steam cranes there simmering in the summer evening heat waves. The big gas tanks throw back an echo of 4017's voice.

We pound through Malden depot and look ahead to the grade crossing at Oak Grove; the gates are down. We call across to the engineer: "OK on the gates!" His raised hand signifies that he's heard us. In Oak Grove, we glimpse a local freight-train crew putting their train together to head into Boston. Lanterns bob highballs in the gathering dusk.

Taking advantage of the reduction in grade, the 4017 picks up some speed. We make a run for Wyoming, and a good thing we do, for our speed drops off again winding up through suburban Melrose and Melrose Highlands. By the time we get between Melrose Highlands and Greenwood the 4017 has settled down to a slow, measured tread. We get a wave from the gate tenders at all the crossings along this stretch, and the headlights of standing autos light up our running gear as we pound by.

Topping the grade at Greenwood we head down toward Crystal Lake, picking up speed. The interlocking signal at Wakefield Junction shows High Green; we call out its indication. Now we're moving, and we slam down past the Green order board on Wakefield Junction station. Train is on a wide curve, so that we can look back on our side along the whole length of the train until it's through the curve and straightening out. We call out, "All black! Green eye on the buggy!" and about that time we're into Wakefield station and out again. The 4017's stubby pilot whips over Albion Street and Chestnut Street to the sound of echoes off the buildings along the right of way.

A few more minutes of this running and we see a gleam along the rails from the three-arm pole at Reading. To reflect on the reflections a moment, remember that we're closing in on the searchlight type of signal that has replaced the long-gone semaphore type of Home Signal, even though the name has stuck—a "three-arm pole." We see a Green over two Reds, the "proceed" indication. We call out, "High Green!"

In less time than it takes for these reflections we rush past Reading station and soon are by Reading Highlands engine house, where we glimpse a number of engines contentedly percolating there in the darkness, their front ends sticking out toward the turntable. They'll haul the commuter trains into Boston tomorrow morning. This is the roundhouse where my grandfather had his experience with a sleepwalking engine that tied up the whole house.

Gramp was night watchman at the Reading Highlands house back in 1926 or maybe '27. He usually had a houseful of engines for next day's commuter trains. They sat there all night with fires banked and steam low. About 4:30 in the morning grandfather would go around, from engine to engine, and stir up the fires and crack open the blowers a little to build up steam gradually for the morning rush.

On one early morning he had done this chore, and all the engines were warming up. However, one of them had been sitting there all night with its throttle notched open just a hair. So long as the fire was banked it didn't have steam enough to move, but grandpa's stirring up the fires made a difference. This engine came to life and walked out of the house into the turntable pit before my grandfather could get to her and stop her.

This jammed the turntable and, therefore, the whole house full of engines. They had to send out a whole string of engines from Boston to take care of the morning trains, and send in the "big hook" itself to get grandfather's sleepwalker out of the pit and things back to normal. After that they always triggered the engines with a short length of chain under the drivers.

Back to BP-5, where we are rolling into less-settled country now. Even so, there are numerous grade crossings for which No. 4017 howls two long and two short whistle blasts. Our headlight bores a hole in the gathering darkness ahead.

Because our long, labored climb upgrade called for steam, and steam calls for coal, it's time to pull the first slide over the stoker pit. We get down off our seat onto the apron and open the bottom section of the coal gate. Using a coal hook, we grope for the grab hole in the slide. Finding it, we jerk this slide forward; coal from the pile runs down into the stoker worm. This chore done, we go to the icebox in the tank leg for a pull at the water jug. Then we lean out the gangways for a spell and look the train over on the curves. No hotboxes: "All black!"

High Green at Wilmington Junction. This is where the branch comes in from Wilmington on the New Hampshire Division. For some obscure reason, it's known as the "Wildcat." It's the route we'll take on the way back tomorrow night. They put the inbound freights down that way over the New Hampshire into Boston because this routing brings them to the upper end of the hump yard at Mystic.

Another three-arm pole comes at us out of the dark at Lowell Junction, showing High Green. The Lowell Junction Branch cuts across here into the New Hampshire Division, entering Lowell Yard at a place—station—called Bleachery. This is an important branch, heavily traveled by the B&M's "cross-country jobs," so called, the symbol freights westbound from Portland to Worcester, Concord and Mechanicville. This is also the route of the summer tourist trains: the *Bar Harbor*, the *State of Maine Express* and the *East Wind*. The Lowell Junction tower operator motions us a highball as we roll by, using the lamp hanging over his desk. "Green order board. Highball from the tower!" we sing out.

Now we have to be on the lookout for No. 178 inbound. This train has a stop at Ballardvale to pick up and let off passengers, and we can't go through there if they are in the station. They are due out of Ballardvale at 8:35; it's that time now. Engineer shuts off a little. Everybody watches for a headlight. There it is. Both engineers dim headlights twice as a signal to come ahead. Passenger cars flip past, light from the windows streaking below our cab window. We look at their hind end. Two red tail lights, the markers, wink at us through the smoke, and there is a red lantern hung on a chain across the platform. As we pick up again to run down toward Lawrence let's give a thought to those markers.

Rule book says that "a train is an engine or more than one engine coupled with or without cars and displaying markers." This is why these marker lights—lamps with red and green bullseyes—were always displayed in their proper place on the hind end of every train, even in the daytime when they were put up but not lighted. At night they showed red to the rear and green to the front and sides, unless the train was in the clear in a siding, when the markers were turned to display green to the rear.

A Yellow Green indication whips by. On the next signal, a stagger block, it's Yellow Red. The engineer shuts off; the fireman widens on the blower and turns off the stoker. We rumble through Shawsheen depot, the platform lights making kaleidoscopic patterns on the cab roof. There's the board—Bottom Yellow—at the upper end of the lead into Lawrence Yard. We nose down to the switch and No. 4017 obediently turns onto the lead track. The engineer dims the headlight; fireman starts the bell clanging. It's down between 4017's paws. As we drift down past the brewery, BP-5 snakes in behind us. The time is 8:46 P.M.

We have to set off the fourteen Lawrence cars on the head end. As we haul slowly down the lead let's get down on the bottom step of the gangway. When we reckon we are about fourteen cars from the lower end of the yard, we drop off and let the train go on by. Start counting cars . . . . four . . . . five . . . . six—head end still hauling down the yard—eight . . . . nine . . . . ten . . . . they clank by. Give him a three-car motion . . . . swing him up;* here's the cut. When things get stopped we get in between the cars, reach over, close both angle cocks and try the pin. Nope, they're stretched and the knuckles are tight. Give him a back-up motion. We hear the slack running in—ka-lang!—got the pin. Give him a go-ahead and grab a handle. The slack runs back out with a jerk; we're off down the yard, riding the rear box car in the hot dark.

Engine hauls down over a highway crossing and around a curve to where we can't see him. The yard switchman will get the iron; we'll decorate the top so that we can see the engine. When the last car of the cut is clear of the switch into the yard, we swing him up again. The switchman's light says "Back up" and we pass the motion to the engine. Now we rumble back across the switch. We unload at the clearance point, letting our cut-offs shove back into the dark. As the engine comes up we swing a stop motion. Closing only the engine's angle cock this time, we get the head pin just before the slack stretches them. We pull

---

* Make signal to stop.

away, hoses snap apart, the escaping air kicks up the dust.

We pick up six Haverhill cars for the head end; while we are doubling over* onto the train the yard switcher has picked off the buggy and, with it, has tied ten Rigbys on the hind end. Now we have eighty-eight cars. After BP-5 is all put together again, with the air cut in, the 4017 lets out a whoop and we head for her. We hear the air going on and see the car knockers' lights looking them over. The car knockers' lights say "Release." "Whaap, whaap!" says 4017, and we climb up into the cab.

When the car knocker reports all eighty-eight cars working the engineer starts the bell; the crossing gates ahead swing down. With the blower on and the stoker kicking over slowly we start hauling down the long yard lead past the Lawrence passenger station. The jack at the upper switch is Red; we stop just clear of it. Passenger train No. 171 is due out of Lawrence at 9:35, so we'll just sit here and wait for them to go.

While waiting here, you might wonder why, in this part of the pike, the B&M seems to make such aimless turns, swinging off quite abruptly eastward then around north again. A look at the timecard shows that we have gone through Andover, then Lawrence, after which we came to North Andover before going into Haverhill. A look at a map shows that several routes run roughly parallel between Boston and the New Hampshire state line. This is because of the many small railroads which existed in the early years. The Andover & Wilmington Railroad was chartered in 1833. This railroad made connection with the Boston & Lowell at Wilmington. Later, the people of Haverhill decided they would like to get into things and the Andover & Haverhill came into being. Meanwhile, Lawrence was becoming a big textile mill town. The A&H line was *relocated* to run through this city, and the result was the convulsive route which now exists. These little railroads were pushed on to Exeter, then to Dover (N.H.) and finally on to Portland. With this extension through New Hampshire and into Maine, the name "Boston & Maine" came into being. Starting at Portland, the B&M now ran through New Hampshire into the Massachusetts towns of Haverhill, Lawrence and Andover to Wilmington and its connection with the Boston & Lowell, then into Boston on B&L rails. (The route into Wilmington was what we called "the Wildcat.") Later, when this arrangement with the Boston & Lowell went sour, the B&M built its own line into Boston through Reading, Wakefield, Melrose and Malden. Still later on, the Boston & Maine gobbled up the B&L as well as its rival, the Eastern Railroad, and all others. We are now on part of the original B&M. All this history I read somewhere but I hardly ever gave it a thought when I was working the head end of high-wheel freight.

While we have been pondering these things of the past, No. 171 has made it

---

* Switching move wherein the road engine picks up a string of cars and brings them to the train.

6 OUTWARD TRAINS VIA WESTERN ROUTE (EASTWARD).—FIRST-CLASS. TERMINAL A PORTLAND DIVI

STATIONS.	25	⊕169	1029	171	1035	23	175	1037	177	1039	183
	Daily	Ex. Sun.	Sun. only	Ex. Sun.	Sun. only	Ex. Sat.	Ex. Sun.	Sun. only	Ex. Sun.	Sun. only	Ex. Sun.
	Portland	Lawrence	Haverhill	Haverhill	Haverhill	Portland	Haverhill	Reading	Haverhill	Haverhill	Haverhill
	PM	PM	PM	PM	PM	PM	PM	PM	PM	PM	PM
Boston	L 7.30	L 7.50	L 7.55	L 8.40	L 8.45	L 9.30	L 9.40	L 9.55	L10.55	L11.30	L11.55
East Somerville	7.34	7.54	7.59	8.44	8.49	9.34	9.44	9.59	10.59	11.34	11.59
Wellington											
Medford Junction	7.37	7.57	8.01	8 47	8.52	9.37	9.47	10.02	11.02	11.37	12.02
Edgeworth											
Malden		s 7.59	s 8.05	s 8.50	s 8.55		s 9.50	s10.05	s11.05	s11.41	s12.05
Oak Grove								s10.07			s12.07
Wyoming		s 8.03	s 8.09	s 8.53	s 8.58		s 9.55	s10.10	s11.09	s11.44	s12.09
Melrose		s 8.05	s 8.11	s 8.56	s 9.02		s 9.58	s10.13	s11.11	s11.46	s12.13
Melrose Highlands		s 8.08	s 8.14	s 8.58	s 9.05		s10.02	s10.16	s11.14	s11.49	s12.16
Greenwood		s 8.11	s 8.17	s 9.01			s10.05	s10.19	s11.17	s11.53	s12.19
Wakefield Junction	7.43	8.13		9.03	9.09	9.45	s10.08			11.56	12.20
Wakefield	7.46	s 8.15	s 8.21	s 9.06	s 9.11		s10.10	s10.23	s11.21	s11.58	s12.23
Reading		s 8.19	s 8.25	s 9.11	s 9.17	9.48	s10.15	s10.28	s11.26	s12.03	s12.28
Reading Highlands								ᴀ10.31			
North Wilmington		8.26	s 8.32	s 9.18	s 9.25		s10.22		f11.32	s12.11	s12.34
Wilmington Junction				9.20	9.27						
Lowell Junction	7.54	8.30	8.36	9.22	9.29	9.56	10.26		11.36	12.15	12.38
Ballardvale			s 8.38	s 9.24	s 9.31		10.28		11.38	s12.17	e12.40
Andover	7.57	s 8.34	s 8.42	s 9.28	s 9.35		10.32		s11.42	s12.21	s12.44
Shawsheen		K 8.37	f 8.45				K10.35		s11.45	e12.24	e12.47
Lawrence	s 8.04	ᴀ 8.42	s 8.53	s 9.35	s 9.43	10.03	s10.42		s11.50	s12.30	s12.51 / 12.53
North Andover				s 9.38			s10.45		s11.53		s 1.01
Ward Hill											
Bradford										e12.41	e 1.08
Haverhill	s 8.16		ᴀ 9.04	ᴀ 9.47	ᴀ 9.55	10.13	ᴀ10.53		ᴀ12.01	ᴀ12.43	ᴀ 1.10
Atkinson											
Westville											
Plaistow											
Newton Junction	8.24					10.23					
Powwow River											
East Kingston											
Exeter	s 8.35					K10.34					
Newfields											
Rockingham	8.40					10.39					
Newmarket											
Durham	s 8.46										
Madbury											
Dover	s 8.56					s 10.53 / 10.55					
Rollinsford	9.00										
Salmon Falls											
Cummings											
North Berwick	9.07					11.07					
Wells Beach											
Kennebunk	9.17					11.20					
Biddeford	9.27										
Saco											
Old Orchard Beach											
Pine Point											
Scarboro Beach											
P. T. Tower One	9.48					11.43					
Portland, Union Sta.	ᴀ 9.55					ᴀ11.50					
	PM	PM	PM	PM	PM	PM	PM	PM	AM	AM	AM

⊕ Does not handle baggage.

ᴋ Stops to leave passengers from Boston.

Schedule time shown at *Portland Union Station*, for information only.

Employee's timecard showing First Class trains Nos. 171 and 23 (The Gull).

into Lawrence. Now they come stamping by, the P-2 on the head end working full stroke. As they get by us the engineer "hooks her up"† and the fireman puts in a few scoops. We see their smoke light up in the glare from the firebox door.

Our fireman has No. 4017's stoker grumbling now, sending a column of smoke into the sky from our stack. We're watching the Red jack. Hasn't changed yet. Five minutes go by. No. 171 should be through North Andover by now. Still no change. I'm going to the telephone box up by the jack and call Lawrence Tower to find out what's going on. And what do you suppose the dispatcher says? He's going to hold us here for No. 23, the *Gull*, due out of Boston at 9:30 and by here at 10:00. That sets things back quite some. We might as well relax—this is going to be a long night.

Since we have about thirty minutes to stay here, let's get off the engine and go sit on a tie pile away from the heat of the firebox. There's time for another history lesson, but we're more inclined to think about getting cooled off and the long night ahead. After a few minutes we see a headlight coming, westbound! What's this? Looks like one of the cross-country jobs, a diesel on the head end: four units, all FT's, in an A-B-B-A lash-up. They go drifting by and, by the look of it, they're not going to stop in Lawrence. Cars a-bangity-banging. Lots of them. Those cars sure get to rocking! Finally the green eye on the buggy as the hind end goes past. We swing highballs to the boys on the rear platform. They answer. They know they're all right for now. They'll stop in Lowell to set off or pick up before hauling on to the Fitchburg.

After what seems like a long time, a lot of noise down toward Lawrence passenger station tells us the *Gull* is coming. No stop; they come flying by, one diesel on the head end, a Maine Central unit. Pullmans and coaches slap past in a haze of dust, red markers blinking at the rear.

As the noise subsides, we mosey back to No. 4017 and the drone of her stoker and blower. Now that No. 23 is really hiking away to the east and north it's not long before the jack goes Yellow, and we start shaking out the slack. We nose out onto the main line. It's 10:08. BP-5 is moving again, but it will be a while before we build up momentum.

The first block signal is already Double Green by the time we get to it. Soon we're at Ward Hill and dropping down into the Merrimac Valley. We let No. 4017 roll down the grade. Plenty of rumble as we go across the Merrimac bridge and make a run for the High Green above Haverhill station, but the engineer starts pinching them down because we have work to do here. Those seventeen cars on the head end belong here; we'll have to drop off in the dark by the yard lead. Dark it is, too. This is the darkest yard I ever was in.

Swing him up now; here's the cut. You get the switch when he hauls them up, and I'll stumble down in the dark and cut him off when he shoves back. (Hope

---

† Adjusts valve gear, using reverse gear lever.

there's nothing back there on the lead!) When, finally, we tie everything back on and the 4017 starts pumping off brakes we climb aboard and take another swallow from the water jug. Night still hot—looks like lightning off toward Boston. We were in here at 10:25, and it's 10:38 when our engineer whistles off. Let's hope we can keep it up. The sooner we get to Rigby, the sooner we hit the hay.

Blower roaring, stoker groaning, the 4017 digs in again. It's time to pull another slide over the stoker worm back in the tank. That done, we hang out the gangways for a bit, looking things over on each side. "All black!"

No. 4017 has gained her stride again, and Atkinson and Plaistow, N.H., storm by. Newton Junction shows a Green order board. Powwow River and East Kingston are woke up by 4017's lusty whistle notifying each grade crossing that the big machine is coming. All signals are Green. The *Gull* is way ahead.

Close to 11:00 P.M. now—we're storming into Exeter, and in another five miles is Rockingham, where we'll get rid of the eight gondolas. The station at Exeter is still lit up because westbound No. 82, the *State of Maine,* makes a stop there at 11:19. We get our train through there in plenty of time. While we're squeezing them down for Rockingham, we watch for No. 82. There's a headlight coming. No. 82 rushes past just as the High Green at Rockingham comes into sight.

If we had time to think about it, the *State of Maine* is one of the through passenger trains running between Maine vacationland and the big cities, leaving Ellsworth in the morning at 11:45 (with a bus connection from Bar Harbor). They make Rockland at 4:10 P.M., Portland at 9:30. We have just seen them through Rockingham, a mite after 11:00. They'll take the Lowell Junction Branch west, then up through North Chelmsford, west again over the Stoney Brook Branch, then down southerly through Clinton to Worcester, from which point the New Haven RR takes them on into New York. No. 82 ordinarily has three or four sleepers plus coaches. In the heavy travel season it sometimes runs in sections, not that we have time to think about it with all the jumping around we do here at Rockingham.

As soon as 4017 slows down enough, I drop off to make the cut. You unload at the switch, ready to get it and send him and the gons back into the siding, where, by then, I'll be. By the time I hit the dirt, 4017 lets go with a "waaaa-wa-wa-wa," ordering a flagman back. I pull the pin and send the cut back up to you. Back in. Stop. Here we go! I pull the pin on the tank, grab a handle and go high. 4017 chuffs out of the siding and on to the water plug. Much clang and clatter as I pry open the covers and pull the water spout down to feed into the manhole. I lean on the valve lever; an eighteen-inch column of water thunders into the tank.

When we have enough water, the spout gets pulled up and swung back into place. I slam down the covers and make back-up motions. The 4017 clumps back to mate hands with our train. Four long blasts ring out, ordering in the flag. Air cuts in, pumps race. Way back in the night we see highballs. BP-5 gets under way at 11:17.

Eleven and a half miles and seventeen minutes later we're calling out, "High Green!" Green order board shows at Dover. We slow to a crawl to pull through town and up past the engine house a mile beyond. We have twenty-five cars to set off here, and this will take some time because they're behind the six Biddefords. Also, the main line curves to the right here, making it necessary to work on the fireman's side of the train and, what's more, spread out along the far side of the westbound main. However, the night has at last cooled off some; our sweaty clothes begin to feel clammy.

After the cut is made, we all swing "Go-ahead" motions and grab handles in the dark. The switch into the yard is tower controlled, so we pull way up past the signals and get the outfit stopped. Just as we get a Yellow jack to let us back into the yard, a headlight shows on the westbound main. "Hot rail!" So everything comes to a stop while we duck out of the way. We stand around waiting for this westbound move to get by. It turns out to be PB-4 (the "other side" of our job) with No. 4011 doing the hauling.

PB-4 seems to take its time hauling down, but that's because their crew has to set out on the other side. We make our delayed move at last—back in, cut off behind six, double over onto twenty-seven more—but it's 12:10 A.M. before we're in one piece and going out of town.

Now the thirty-two miles to go before our next stop is all over well-ballasted heavy rail, so we should be able to make some time! We pull more stoker slides and work some with the coal maul back in the tank. Another pull at the water jug and lean out each gangway to look 'em over.

High Green at Rollinsford—the Conway Branch cuts off here toward the White Mountains—then a bridge over the Piscataqua into Maine. Seven miles more to another High Green at North Berwick, where the route from Portsmouth used to join the main line. It's 12:27 when we're through North Berwick, and we begin to get some sea fog now. The damp makes our sticky clothes more uncomfortable, but things are looking better, even so.

Here's another curve. Take a look along the right-hand side. Oh, oh! What's that? We're quickly back on straight iron, but I thought I saw a flash of fire about fifteen or twenty cars behind. The next time we enter a right-hand curve everyone is looking. There it is! Quite far back. That's a hot one for sure. Well, there goes our run.

Engineer goes for the air and shuts off. We gather up what packing tools we can find on the engine and, as soon as our speed is down, unload in the dark and strike out toward the hind end. We keep giving a go-ahead motion to get the engineer to help us by closing up the distance to the flamer, which we now see clearly. As the train clanks to a stop the 4017 blows out a flag.

Here it is, on a box car. When we snap up the journal cover the flames really surge up. We start digging out the flaming waste and smothering it with ballast

For steam buffs, a pretty sight at Dover, N. H.

and dirt. The conductor shows up, also with tools and a bag full of sticks of journal dope.

Once the fire's put out, we begin packing the box full of dope and cooling things off. We know for sure that we're going to have to set this baby off at the first side track, which is at Wells Beach. Once she's cool enough to move, conductor tells us to have the engineer haul along to Wells at about ten miles an hour; he will ride the car to make the cut. We hike for the head end. It was 12:35 when we stopped; it's 12:45 now. Seven minutes more to get to the engine and call in the flag. Four minutes more for him to get on.

At 12:56 we take the slack and start the long, slow pull, and it's 1:30 before we make Wells. The conductor makes the cut thirty cars deep when we stop. You stay ten cars back of the engine. I'll be back another ten or fifteen cars. Flag is whistled out again. What with hauling up, getting the switch and the derail, shoving back into the siding, cutting off and hauling out, we lose another thirteen minutes.

While we put the train together the conductor sets the hand brake on the cripple and phones the dispatcher from the box on the three-arm pole, giving him the car number and any other info. he needs to know. Ten minutes more. As we walk back to the head end, four long blasts start the flagman in. Five minutes more before plain and fancy highballs wave from the rear, making the time about 2:00 A.M. when at last the 4017 yelps, "Gone from here!" Minute by minute our long night is getting longer.

Now the fog is setting in solid. Everything is getting wet. We wish we were in Rigby. Perhaps *this* time we'll get over the road. Fog doesn't allow us to see very far, but we keep watching the train in the prescribed manner.

But what's this ahead? A Yellow Green! Now what? The stagger block for Kennebunk emerges through the fog. Yellow Red. Once again shut off, kick in the blower; we mine some more coal back in the tank. We crawl along to the three-arm pole at Kennebunk and by the time we get there, sure enough, it's All Red. We grind to a stop clear of the signal. I unload and head for the phone box. The flag goes out again. What the dispatcher tells me is disheartening. He has a passenger train, a camp extra, coming up behind us, eastbound, and he's running them around us. He has to cross them over here at Kennebunk because there's a westbound freight high-wheeling out of Biddeford.

Here we are, stuck again. It's 2:15, foggy and damp. The headlight pushes a long shaft out ahead. The headlight generator whines; the fireman cuts back the blower and works over the fire with his chisel-shaped slice bar, breaking up clinkers and stirring it up.

2:20 comes and goes. 2:25—no sign of anybody yet. Then the eastbound signal on the opposite main goes Middle Green. At 2:27 a headlight punches through the fog and a pair of diesels, showing white indicators and hauling a half-dozen sleepers, coasts by us and into the crossovers up ahead. We come alive again.

Fireman widens on the blower, gets the stoker to grumbling again. Call in the flag. We'll have to hope he gets on. (Can't see the hind end in the fog.) At 2:34 we get a Yellow Red, which turns to Yellow Green even before we start moving. We shake out the slack about 2:37. No. 4017 stumbles on the wet rail. Spread sand on the rail and try again.

We're just about moving when the westbound freight shows up, its diesels accelerating. They have been coming along slowly, held down by restrictive signal indications. Now their cars hammer by in the fog and dark. We barely see their wild highballs swung from the rear platform.

Nine miles to Biddeford, and there we set off the six head cars, pick up eighteen, and it's 3:00 A.M. before we get out of there. Before long morning's grey light will begin to show. We're tired, and cold, and dirty. The fog turns to a drizzle of rain. Old Orchard Beach drops behind. Pine Point is next. All we want now is to get in. Hope there's a track for us in Rigby.

Here's Scarboro Beach; we start looking through the wet for signals that will help or hinder. There—a Yellow Green. A short time later, a Yellow Red stagger block. Now everyone is looking . . . . there it is! Bottom Yellow. We're heading in. PT Tower 1 gives us a highball, and we haul into Rigby Yard, creeping down the lead. At 3:35 A.M. we're glad it's over. We pull the head pin and let the air go with a final blast. BP-5 is in. By the time we get 4017 headed for the house the first grey light is brightening the drizzly sky. Now to the buggy, to a wash-up —and the bunk.

Side labels: **TERMINAL DIVISION** (upper rows) · **NEW HAMPSHIRE DIVISION** (lower rows)

Miles from Boston	Passing Sidings Cap. Cars	STATIONS	3001 Sun. only Concord	1 Ex. Sun. Woodsville	①303 Ex. Sun. Concord	H 3303 Ex. Sat. and Sun. Wilmin'n	H×345 Ex. Sat. and Sun. Wilmin'n	3305 Ex. Sun. Lowell	H×347 Ex. Sat. and Sun. Wilmin'n	3307 Ex. Sun. Lowell	5 Daily C.P.R.	360… Ex. S.. Conco..
			A M	A M	A M	A M	A M	A M	A M	A M	A M	A M
		Boston W N X L	L 1.10	L 1.45	L 5.00	L 5.35	6.28	L 6.40	L 6.50	L 7.40	L 8.00	
1.85		Mystic Junction T N X	1.15	1.50	5.05	5.42	6.33	6.45	6.55	7.45		8.05
2.42		Winter Hill X										
2.81		Somerville Junction T	1.17				6.35	6.47		7.47		
3.56	53	North Somerville T			s 5.03	f 5.45						
4.01		Tufts College						s 6.50				
4.58		Medford Hillside										
5.48		West Medford T	1.20	1.54	s 5.12	s 5.49	6.37	s 6.53	6.59	s 7.50		8.09
7.34		Wedgemere T				5.52		6.56				
7.82	29	Winchester T N	s 1.25	1.57	s 5.18	s 5.54	6.40	s 6.58	7.02	s 7.55		8.12
8.95		Cross Street				s 5.57		e 7.01				
9.45		Woburn Highlands				s 5.59		s 7.02				
9.96		Woburn W				s 6.03		s 7.05		s 8.00		
10.97		Central Square				6.05						
12.18		North Woburn				s 6.07		f 7.09				
9.00		Winchester Highlands T										
9.76		Montvale T	1.28	1.59	5.21		6.42		7.04			8.14
10.35		Grape Street										
10.96		Oakland										
11.37		Lindenwood										
11.84		Farm Hill X										
		Pleasant Street X										
12.10		Stoneham T W X										
10.48		Walnut Hill T										
12.74		South Wilmington T										
13.97		North Woburn Jct. T	1.33		5.26	6.10	6.47	7.12	7.09	8.08		
15.20	39	Wilmington T D	c 1.35	2.05	s 5.30	A 6.13	A 6.49	s 7.15	A 7.11	s 8.11		8.19
16.60		Silver Lake			5.35							
19.22		East Billerica										
21.79		North Billerica T	u 1.48	2.11	s 5.42							
23.32		South Lowell X						s 7.24		8.18		8.25
24.66	49	Bleachery T N X			s 5.48							
25.55		Lowell N	s 1.55 / 1.57	s 2.16 / 2.30	s 5.52 / 6.01			A 7.30		A 8.25	s 8.30 / 8.32	
27.28	148	Middlesex T W X										
28.55		North Chelmsford X	2.02	2.35	s 6.08							8.37
32.11		Tyngsboro T	2.06	2.39	s 6.15							
38.96		Nashua, Union Sta. T D X	s 2.14 / 2.35	s 2.48 / 3.02	s 6.26 / 6.32						s 8.48 / 8.51	
40.78		Tie Plant	2.39	3.06	6.36							8.55
46.09		Merrimack T	u 2.45		s 6.43							
47.78		Reeds Ferry T										
53.94		South Manchester T	2.52	3.19	6.52							9.07
55.68	155	Manchester T W N X	s 2.55 / 3.20	s 3.22 / 3.35	s 6.55 / 7.05						s 9.10 / 9.15 [3601]	L 9.1
57.90		Amoskeag	3.24	3.39	7.09						9.19	9.2
64.37		Hooksett T			s 7.21							
71.30		Bow X	3.38	3.53	7.30						9.33	9.3
73.32		Concord W N X	A 3.45	A 4.00	A 7.35						A 9.38	A 9.4
			A M	A M	A M	A M	A M	A M	A M	A M	A M	A M

No. **3001** will leave from "A" House at 12.55 a.m. for North Station.

① No. **303** Saturdays and Holidays run via Woburn Loop, "S" Woburn 5.23 a.m.

No. **3303** make regular stop opposite Power House at Engine Terminal.

H   Will not run May 30, June 17, July 4, Sept. 7.
c   Stop to leave employes.
u   Stop to leave newspapers only.
×   Does not carry passengers.

(81)

Employee's timecard for chapter following. Train No. 5 is Alouette.

9 New Hampshire Division

WE SAW THE PORTLAND DIVISION—THE HEART OF IT, AT LEAST—FROM THE HEAD END of BP-5. Now let's take a look at the New Hampshire Division, in daylight, from the rear of BU-3. This time we won't do the work, but assume that we've wangled passes to ride as deadheading observers.

BU-3 ran from Boston to White River every morning. Our trip this morning is in the Fall and the weather is starting to turn cold. The crew was called for duty at 6:45 A.M. We join them soon after. Our train is stretched out down through Yard 9 at Mystic so that the buggy, No. C-18, is way around under the bridges near Sullivan Square. The crew has already looked 'em over for brakes, retainers and so forth. As we hike down we see our diesels, three units, coming over the High Line: Nos. 4204-A, 4204-B and 4217-A. The head-end man and the car knocker will hook them on. We continue our long hike to the buggy.

There we see that the markers are hanging out and smoke from the stove coming out of the stack; the flagman has a cosy fire going. We greet the conductor. These formalities over, we climb aboard. We learn that they have eighty-one cars and the caboose. There are ten Lowells on the head pin, then eight Manchesters, twenty-three Concords, fifteen Central Vermonts and twenty-five Canadian Pacifics. With all this stuff we are going to need a shove over the hump; one of the yard diesels has already gone down toward Yard 21 to cross over and come on behind.

With the engines on and the air pumped up, BU-3 gets a brake test. The pusher bangs on behind (no need this time to hook in the air). As No. 3307 goes by Mystic, about 7:45, our slack goes clanging out, the pusher opens up with a businesslike rumble, shoving the slack in again, and we're on our way. Our head end is passing the hump as we roar under the last bridge and into Yard 9. We're out on the rear platform with the flagman, who holds the pin pulled on the rear knuckle.

As the pusher bulldozes us up by the hump, we exchange highballs with Mystic Tower and shout a few remarks to some of the gang near the yard office. Then the pusher shuts off and drops away. Hang on! The slack is about to run out with a jerk. No. 304 goes inward on the High Line, the cold air turning its exhaust steam to clouds of white. We seem to have the jack because we're going right along.

Ball signal, diamond and B&M train at White River Junction

Soon we whip-snap out onto the main line at Winter Hill, so let's go inside and get warm. Here's Somerville Junction, where the Hill Crossing freight cutoff comes in. We're away through North Somerville. At Tufts College, No. 3312 goes by in a cloud of steam and the flagman flips them a highball. The conductor is busy working on his bills; the flagman is busy getting motions from the crossing tenders° at West Medford. Other inward trains slam by at intervals. We lose track of them, but the boys on the head end won't, because we're not supposed to go through Wedgemere if a train is making a station stop there.

Winchester now, and we raise a dust through the station. Highball from the tower. Hang on—we're moving right along! The Woburn Loop branches off to the left. The head end is up near Winchester Highlands. High Green at Montvale, where the Stoneham Branch swings to the right. Quite crisp out on the platform now; somehow we all crowd into the monitor. We go past the chemical and fertilizer plants at South Wilmington. The slack runs in as head end pinches 'em down a mite just as No. 3312 clears the crossovers at Wilmington.

North Woburn Junction—where Woburn Loop comes back in again on the left—and then Wilmington. Green order board. Now for a long ride during which we see traces of the old Middlesex Canal. After a spell, Billerica Shop lies to our left, followed by North Billerica, where the Lexington (Bedford) Branch comes in, also on the left.

Now the air is going on and the head end is pulling down to the yard switch at South Lowell. It is a hand-thrown switch (though it will later become an electric one controlled by Lowell Tower). We nearly stop, but then the slack is jerked out and we haul down slowly. The hind end is in yard limits, so there's no flagging as long as we get the whole train in before No. 305 is due.

Though we can't see what's going on up ahead, we know that the cut is being made behind the ten Lowells. These are hauled up and the yard crew pulls the head pin. Then they send the diesels down through a clear alley to hook up to our train again. We move in further and a second cut is made behind the eight Manchesters. During this last haul in we cleared the switch; the flagman straightens up the iron.

With the Manchesters, the diesels back onto our Lowell pick-ups, which are seven CV's and six Concords. Now we have eighty-nine cars including the hack. No. 305 comes past as we're getting an air test. The conductor gets the bills. The flagman has a coffeepot on the stove, secured by a wire looped around the stovepipe. We're set to go—hang on!—the slack is coming.

We pull up through the interlocking, a mechanical one operated by Bleachery Tower. Lowell Junction Branch to the right. Green order board. Highball from the Tower. New Haven wye on the left. Highball from Hale Street tower. Green order board on Lowell depot. Highballs from crossing tenders. We're gone from

---

° Rule book says "gate tenders" or "crossing watchmen," but they were "crossing tenders" to us.

here, the sound of the train echoing off the gas works as we rumble by. Soon Middlesex engine house is on the left and the Merrimac River on the right. We glimpse a sign marking the beginning of the long-gone Middlesex Canal. Then North Chelmsford Tower, a Green order board, and a wye where the Stoney Brook Branch takes off to the left.

Let's go in for a while and have some coffee as we ramble north at a good clip. As we lean into a curve at Tyngsboro we're all over on the right-hand side, for this is one of the few places where we can see the entire length of the train—or a train of a hundred cars, if we had that many!

Here's Nashua. A reverse curve, so hang on tight to the rear platform rail. Green order board. Highballs all over the place. Nashua was once a busy junction with the WN&P,✻ but is now just a terminal for the stubby, freight-only line to Hillsboro. With a final whip-snap we're out of the curve, over a bridge, and stretching out toward the Koppers tie-creosoting plant off to the right. Through Merrimac, where a spur that we called the "Souhegan Railroad" lies on the left. After awhile we're rumbling across a steel bridge over the Merrimac at Goff's Falls—and braking heavily, for the head end is hauling in at South Manchester. This long yard lead lets us get all the way in, and Manchester Tower throws the iron behind us.

When we stop, the flagman and conductor start walking up, one on each side, feeling the journals as they go. The head end will set off the eight Manchesters and, while we're here, No. 5 comes breezing by, brake shoes smoking, and with a fancy, classic observation car on the rear. After they're gone, our slack runs out. The crew grabs a handle on the rear and we're soon slipping over the many grade crossings up to Amoskeag, the mills lying on the left. Another big left-hand curve at Martin's, where we can see clear to the head end, our diesels and a haze of exhaust smoke. A long, fast ride through Hooksett, then Bow, where we see the Suncook Valley iron coming in from the right to run beside us into Concord.

Braking sharply now, the head end is coming down to a Bottom Yellow at Concord. We pull slowly in and way up on the back side of the yard. When we're stopped, the head-end man cuts behind the seven CV's on the head pin and they're pulled way up by the diamond. Now the yard crew goes to work with an 0–6–0 switcher, picking off our Concords and CV's and finally putting back eight CP's, our Boston CV's and six Concord CV's. When these are out of the way they whistle our head end back with three long blasts, and our head end ties on, giving us twenty-eight CV's on the head pin followed by thirty-seven CP's on the rear.

Meanwhile, the conductor has been in the yard office swapping waybills and getting orders. He gives the head-end man a set of duplicates and comes back to the buggy with the rest. All train orders are addressed to the conductor and engineer. Ours read:

✻ Worcester, Nashua & Portland RR.

C&E Eng. 4204

Engine 4204 run extra Concord to White River Jct.

Not protecting against extra trains.
Wait at Canaan until 12:15 twelve fifteen PM

This order and a clearance form lets us go, now showing white flags at the prescribed place on the engine. We are to meet No. 320, but the meet will not be fixed by the dispatcher. No. 320 is a First Class train, and in the timecard; thus we will fix our own meet.

The usual brake test, and then we hear them whistle off up ahead. The slack jerks out; we move. There are four balls on the signal at the diamond and we get a highball from the car knocker under Free Bridge, another one from the switchman by the ball signal. From here we can see back into the large, dark train shed at the passenger station. As we hammer over the diamond we can see another ball signal back near the station. Now we're running on single iron.

Inside to eat some lunch and have more coffee, which tastes good and warming—that Concord yard is the coldest place in the world. Penacook comes next; if we look sharp on the left we may glimpse the old Woodstock Ry. engine that switches the Stratton flour mill there. Green order board. Through Boscawen and Gerrish the miles clack away, though not so fast now. It's uphill going. Southbound signals obediently clear up behind us as we leave each block. Northbound ones stand out behind us, signaling an authoritative: "STOP. BU-3 is ahead of you."

Speed slacks off still more. The head end is well into the grade now, and the further we go, the slower we go until, as we pass Franklin, we're right down to an amble. But the diesel motors aren't ambling; they are leaning into the grade—three sets of engines roaring to the heavens against the pull on their rear drawbar. Green order board at Franklin. On and up we climb.

As we near Halcyon, with the head end almost over the top, we begin to speed up. Here's Halcyon. Red order board, which brings the conductor out on the platform to snare the order off the fork on the pole. The order reads:

C&E Eng. 2728

Engine 2728 work extra between White River
and Canaan not protecting against extra trains

except protects against Extra 4204 North after 12:15
twelve fifteen PM. Extra 4204 gets this order at
Halcyon.

The "flimsy" is passed around, read and understood.
We hold our speed through Andover and Potter Place, but it's short-lived be-

Standard Train Order Blank for 19 Order.

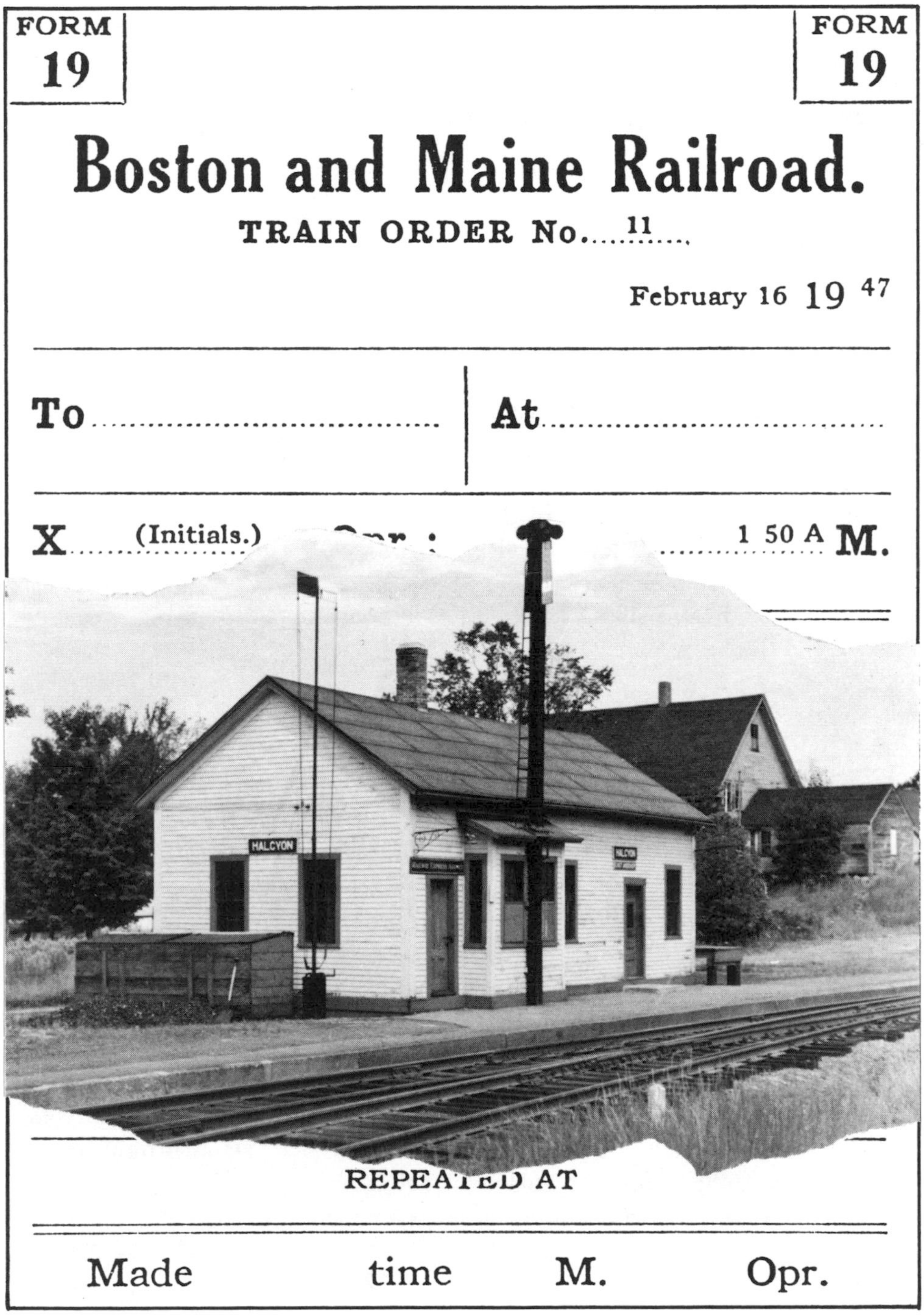

FORM 19		FORM 19

Boston and Maine Railroad.

TRAIN ORDER No....11....

February 16 19 47

To .... | At ....

X........ (Initials.) .... 1 50 A M.

REPEATED AT

Made   time   M.   Opr.

Here's Halcyon.   And a specimen 'flimsy.'

cause we start to slow for Gale. This is where we will meet No. 320. Gale siding holds eighty-three cars; we have sixty-six. The next siding that can hold us is Grafton, but we can't make there against 320, so we're stuck here. We slow to an almost stop and then the slack stretches as we crawl in. Flagman drops off and straightens the iron, trots along and gets back on. Presently the slack runs in; we stop. All is quiet.

We'll be here for awhile. It's not the time of year to pick blackberries along the right of way, so let me tell you something that happened here. There was that student brakeman from White River making his first trip as a student. As we waited here for No. 313, he asked:
"Who closes the switch when we pull out?"
"Flagman does," instructed the conductor.
"What if we *don't* stop, and the flagman can't make it back on?"
The conductor looked at him and said, "Whenever you get off here in these wilds, take a brake club with you. We had a flagman clawed to death by wildcats when he got left behind."
Wildcats. You could see the kid imagining himself versus a pack of wildcats, with only a brake club for defense, while the marker lights of his train disappear down the track. But he finished the job, and what happened to him I've told elsewhere in this book. Some of us could be rather rough on students.

Now a distant whistle echoes through the hills. No. 320 is coming right on time. We leave the stove and go out on the rear end. The whistle again, closer now, and we see smoke coming up toward our head end. Ha—there they go in a flurry of dust, engine No. 3662 striding out for Bean Town trailing a milk car, express car, baggage car, combine and coach. They'll get more cars at Concord. A highball from our head end; our slack runs out with a crash and we're moving before 320's markers are out of sight behind.
As we haul out of the siding the flagman gets the iron, then makes his run for the hind end. (No brake club, you know.) We stop for him, however, but get going again soon. All set now, up through Converse we clack. The scenery is great in the sharp, clear air. Then on through a place I always heard called "Gungawam." I spell it the way it sounded because I never saw it in print or ever knew where the name came from. To go through this territory on a cold, clear night was something! You could reach up and pick the stars right out of the sky, provided the Northern Lights didn't get in the way.
Now comes Danbury with a Green order board, then Grafton with its 110-car siding, then in another two miles, Cardigan. Mt. Cardigan is off there to the right. We keep right on to Canaan. The time is 12:45 P.M. Green order board. A local is over on the siding—engine No. 2728—and no worry about us for them, now that we're by. We're dropping down grade now and beginning to hike. Five

miles more to Pattee, and two more from there to Enfield, where BU-1, the night job, regularly sets off a milk car.

This reminds me of a night I was on BU-1, when we were just ahead of No. 325, that train we often spoke of as "three-and-a-quarter." Our engineer was a fast runner, also a slightly don't-give-a-damn type of guy. Our milk car was on the head pin and we had to get rid of it at Enfield, as above. We had it all figured out how we'd make the setoff and go into White River *ahead* of 325. The fireman joined me on the ground, running around throwing switches and derails and winding up hand brakes. Well, we set off that milk car in record time; our engineer was whistling in the flag almost at the time I was pulling the pin on the milk track and our flagman was planting a fusee and starting back for a grab onto the train. Engineer tied on, whistled off, and we left town! When he realized that the flagman had planted a fusee, he roared, "What did he do that for? It'll stop three-and-a-quarter for sure!" Conductor had some things to say, too, because we figured 325 was *that* close behind us. We went on down the hill like a stone dropping down a well, and were already pulling around the wye at White River when we heard 325 hammering down after us. Never did know whether they saw the fusee or not.

OK, back to BU-3. We're rounding Mascoma Lake. We can look ahead to the head end, with which we swap highballs, and we're all set for a nice ride along the Mascoma River through Lebanon. We can tell that the diesels are on the dynamic brake because the slack is all bunched up. We move slower and slower, past the Westboro engine house and out onto the Connecticut River bridge, coming to a halt, finally, at the STOP post on the Vermont side. When we start again, we know that two balls are showing at the diamond and the diesels are groaning into the Central Vermont RR yard. We decorate the rear end and shout remarks to the guys hanging around the station.

When we stop in the CV yard, the flagman takes the CV bills and has to hike up twenty-eight cars to cut the air and pull the pin between the CV's and the CP's. Then he'll take the bills to the yard office, while at the head end they pull the pin there and the air goes out of the CV's with a roar. The diesels come back through a clear alley and a switchman motions them down against our hind end. The big nose of No. 4204 dwarfs our buggy.

Once the air is cut in again, the engine crew changes cabs. When they get a motion from the switchman, the diesels rev up and we start hauling back past the White River depot toward Nutt Street and the B&M yard. When we've hauled in far enough, the diesels cut off—the air in what's left of BU-3 going out with a wham—to mosey back to the Westboro roundhouse. A switcher picks up the buggy.

We have completed our trip over the backbone of the New Hampshire Division. The switcher nudges the buggy onto the caboose track. We hear a whistle —from way down on the Connecticut River line—echoing off the hills.

Milk Job

In my time the Boston & Maine did considerable business with milk trains, most of it over Fitchburg Division and the Cheshire Branch to connections with the Rutland. However, the only milk jobs in my experience were Nos. 351 and 352 on the New Hampshire Division between Boston and White River Junction. We'd go up from Boston at night as No. 351, basically a freight train like BU-1. The next night we came down as No. 352, all milk cars, at passenger-train speed. The contract called for those cars to be set over at Rutherford Avenue in Charlestown by a certain time in the early morning, so nothing laid out the milk train if possible.

The buggy on these jobs was one of the long wooden ones that rode well at high speed. At White River it was always spotted "uptown" near the passenger station instead of down on the buggy track. Anyway, it was uptown where the job went to work.

The job went on duty at White River somewhere about 7:00 P.M., as I recall. Our connection came down from St. Albans on the Central Vermont. We'd listen for the CV engine whistling up beyond the yard. Then, as soon as the CV job came in, our conductor would beat it over to the passenger station to get the waybills and the orders. The big CV steamer was cut off and the switcher grabbed our buggy and swapped it for the CV one. Our diesel was usually idling away out on the Connecticut River bridge. Once the CV engine was out of the way, our engine clunked back across the diamond for a hitch.

Car knockers' lights bobbed about looking 'em over and, as soon as we had an air test (the waybills and orders letting us go), the diesels rapped off two blasts. With highballs from the switchman at the diamond, No. 352 was off for Boston. Running time was fast because the milk cars rode on passenger-car trucks, and

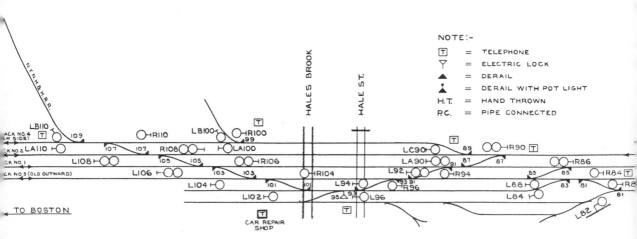

tonnage was light. Oftentimes we'd see the big highway milk trucks coming down over the road, and exchange salutes with them—they, who eventually took the contracts away from the railroad!

At Concord we were run right into the train shed of the passenger station. Here we unloaded some Concord cans from the "peddler car" just ahead of the buggy in the usual milk-train make-up. I don't clearly remember, but maybe we set off a Concord car, too. Perhaps some old-timer knows.

We did set off a car at Lowell. It was on the head pin at Lowell, and we'd cut behind it, take it down by Lowell Tower and leave it. Then the tower put us back onto our train at the Lowell passenger station. While the set-off was taking place the boys on the rear, along with the station crowd, were getting rid of the Lowell cans from the peddler.

Once when I had the head end of No. 352 we were doing this work at Lowell. After leaving the Lowell car, I came back onto the train with the engine, hooked everything up and looked back for a highball. I seemed to see an extraordinary amount of excitement back near the rear end, but no highball. I went back to see what was going on.

What had happened was that as we came sailing around the curve into Lowell station the head truck of the last milk car derailed just before it got to Middlesex Street crossing. It struck the blacktop grading at Middlesex Street, blasting a hole one could crawl into. Then the truck rerailed itself. Needless to say, it just about scared the life out of the crossing tender, and the noise brought a sizable crowd from all directions. Blacktop and timbers from the crossing lay scattered everywhere. We looked the truck over carefully but found no damage; also no damage to the track except for a few splintered ties. No one knows why it happened. We were exceedingly lucky.

Diagram of switches and signals, Lowell, Mass., from B&M RR plan ZN-5, Oct. 8, 1947. See Appendix for additional diagrams, New Hampshire Division.

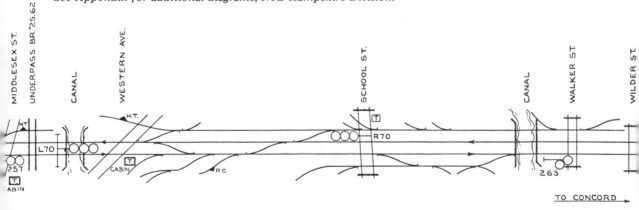

I remember when there were forty-nine trains departing . . .

Passenger Service

In the late 1940s and for quite a while thereafter, the B&M had passenger trains. We saw a few during our recent trip on BP-5. There were many more—in commuter service alone, I remember when there were forty-nine trains departing from North Station on a weekday night between 4:45 and 6:45 p.m. Between these two times there was a train leaving on an average of every two-and-a-half minutes (see Appendix for a list of these trains). All of these trains had to cross the drawbridges over the Charles River just outside the station, whose twenty-four tracks narrowed down to eight tracks across the four bridges. To the forty-nine commuter departures add any inbound trains, plus the drafts backing in from Yards 2, 3 and 4, to have some idea of the "keeping track" job they had to do in Tower "A" situated just over the river.

All of these trains had to cross the drawbridges.

The morning rush hour was just as crowded, and all through the day there were trains for the accommodation of shoppers from out of town.

Besides these locals were quite a few through jobs, with names that bring back memories of train travel when it was commonplace and a taken-for-granted part of railroading. Some of these are listed on page opposite, just as they were printed in the public timetable.

In addition to these were the *Flying Yankee* and the *Minute Man*, also the *Monadnock, Day White Mountains, Connecticut Yankee, Washingtonian, Montrealer, East Wind* and the *Bar Harbors*.

These trains kept a fleet of engines busy. The through jobs used the P-2 and P-3 Pacifics, and the 4100's—4–8–2—when business was heavy, until the diesels came and displaced them. Mostly Moguls and 3600's were used on the locals, and a few 4–4–0's, though these were all but gone by the time I was railroading. There were some 3200's and sometimes a K-7 used on the locals.

WILMINGTON TRAIN

What was a passenger job like? Let's work one; then you'll know. Assume we've been called for a local from Boston to Wilmington and put up, and that we're "qualified to back drafts," a requirement for covering this job. It means that we'll be in charge of the movement of the train, empty, from the storage yards to the North Station.

Jobs varied, as in one case we would have to go to the oil house to get the rear end equipment—a pair of markers, flagging can,* red and white lights and a "riding hose." Other times, this stuff would already be stowed away on the train, either in the combination car or in one of the coach toilets. This Wilmington job is the latter type; no heavy equipment for us to lug.

* Metal box, with shoulder strap, to hold flags.

ALOUETTE No. 5
Canadian Pacific Ry. Buffet Parlor Car
489 Boston to Montreal. Buffet available
to coach passengers.
Coaches: Boston to Montreal.

ALOUETTE No. 20
Canadian Pacific Ry. Buffet Parlor Car
490 Montreal to Boston. Buffet available
to coach passengers.
Coaches: Montreal to Boston.

RED WING
No. 325
Sleeping Cars via B&M-CP: Car CP6 Boston to Montreal. 3 Comp. D.R. Lounge
Buffet. Car CP7 Boston to Montreal.
12 Sec. 2 Double Bedrooms.
Coaches: Boston to Montreal.

RED WING
No. 302
Sleeping Cars via CP-B&M: Car 468
Montreal to Boston. 3 Comp. D.R.
Lounge Buffet. Car 470 Montreal to
Boston. 12 Sec. 2 Double Bedrooms.
Coaches: Montreal to Boston.

NEW ENGLANDER
No. 325
Pullman Sleeping Car CN1 via B&M-CV-CN Boston to Montreal. 12 Sec. 2
Double Bedrooms.
Coaches: Boston to Montreal.

NEW ENGLANDER
No. 302
Pullman Sleeping Car 82 via CN-CV-B&M
Montreal to Boston. 12 Sec. 2 Double
Bedrooms.
Coaches: Montreal to Boston.

AMBASSADOR
No. 307
B&M-CV-CN Parlor Car 307 Boston to
Montreal.
Cafe Grill Car: Boston to Montreal (12 30
p.m. to 9 30 p.m.).
Coaches: Boston to Montreal.

AMBASSADOR No. 332
B&M-CV-CN Parlor Car 38 Montreal to
Boston.
Cafe Grill Car: Montreal to Boston (9 20
a.m. to 6 50 p.m.).
Coaches: Montreal to Boston.

STATE OF MAINE
No. 81
Sleeping Cars may be occupied in Portland until 8 00 am. weekdays.
Pullman Sleeping Cars:
  Car 19 New York GCT to Portland. 6 Comp. 3 D.R.
  Car 20 New York GCT to Portland. 12 Sec. D.R.
  Car 21 New York GCT to Portland. 14 Sec.
  Car 22 New York GCT to Portland. 2 Comp. D.R. 3 Single Bedrooms. Buffet Lounge.
  Car 23 except Saturdays from New York GCT to Concord, NH. 12 Sec. D.R.
Coaches: New York GCT to Portland.
Smoking coach New York GCT to Portland.

No. 82
Pullman Sleeping Cars ready for occupancy at 8 30 pm. in Portland
  and must be vacated on arrival in New York GCT.
  Car 820 Portland to New York GCT. 6 Comp. 3 D.R.
  Car 821 Portland to New York GCT. 12 Sec. D.R.
  Car 822 Portland to New York GCT. 14 Sec.
  Car 823 Portland to New York GCT. 2 Comp. D.R. 3 Single Bedrooms. Buffet Lounge.
  Car 240 except Saturdays (260 Sundays) from Concord, NH to New York GCT. 12 Sec. D.R.
Coaches: Portland to New York GCT.
Smoking coach Portland to New York GCT.

GULL No. 23 via Lewiston
Ready for occupancy in Boston at 9 00 p.m.
Pullman Sleeping Cars: Car 230 Boston to
Bangor. Car 231 Boston to Calais. 12
Sec. D.R. Car 235 Boston to Van Buren.
10 Sec. D.R. 2 Comp. Car 234 Boston
to Halifax. 10 Sec. D.R. 2 Comp. Car
232 Boston to Saint John. 10 Sec. D.R.
2 Comp. Truro to Sydney. 12 Sec. D.R.
Parlor Car: Weekdays Saint John to
Moncton with Buffet service.
Dining Car: Moncton to Halifax. Bangor
to Van Buren.
Coaches: Boston to Saint John, Saint John
to Halifax.
Station stop of 30 minutes at McAdam for
breakfast.

GULL No. 8 via Augusta
Pullman Sleeping Cars: Car 429 Halifax to
Boston. 10 Sec. D.R. 2 Comp. Car 435
Saint John to Boston. 10 Sec. D.R. 2
Comp. Sydney to Truro. 12 Sec. D.R.
Parlor Car: Moncton to Saint John with
Buffet service.
Dining Car: Halifax to Moncton.
Coaches: Halifax to Saint John. St. John
to Boston.

MOUNT ROYAL No. 5502
Pullman Sleeping Cars: Car 78 weekdays from Alburgh to Boston. 12 Sec. D.R. Car 78 Sundays from Burlington 9 50 p.m.
to Boston. 12 Sec. D.R.
Coaches: Daily Montreal to Rutland & Bellows Falls to Boston.
Weekdays Ogdensburg to Boston. Sundays Alburgh to Boston

GREEN MOUNTAIN
No. 5503
Coaches: Boston to Alburgh, Fri., Sat., Sun. and Mon.
Boston to Rutland, Tues., Wed. and Thurs. Daily Rutland
to Montreal.

Nos. 5510 and 5512
Coaches: Alburgh to Boston, Sat., Sun., Mon. and Tues.
Rutland to Boston, Wed., Thurs. and Fri. Daily Montreal
to Rutland.

THE CHESHIRE No. 5505
Streamline Train. All seats reserved. All coach class tickets
honored except those for restricted excursions. No checked
baggage handled on this train. No skis or other winter sports
equipment will be accepted. Buffet service.

No. 5507
Coaches: Boston to Rutland.

MOUNT ROYAL
No. 5511 Weekdays. No. 5557 Sundays
Pullman Sleeping Cars: Car 511 ex. Sat. from Boston to Alburgh
leaving Rutland 4 30 a.m. 12 Sec. D.R. Car 511 Saturdays
only from Boston to Burlington leaving Rutland 4 30 a.m.
and may be occupied in Burlington until 8 00 a.m. 12 Sec. D.R.
Coaches: Daily Boston to Bellows Falls and Rutland to
Montreal. Except Saturdays from Boston to Ogdensburg.
Saturdays from Boston to Alburgh.   9-28-47 IV

KENNEBEC
No. 11 via Augusta

B&M-MC Parlor Car 110 Boston to Bangor. D.R.
Restaurant Lounge Car: Boston to Bangor (9 45 AM
to 3 25 PM).
Deluxe Streamline Coaches: Boston to Bangor.

No. 12 via Augusta
B&M-MC Parlor Car 120 Bangor to Boston. D.R.

Restaurant Lounge Car: Bangor to Boston (1 40 PM
to 7 20 PM).
Dining Car: Van Buren to No. Me. Jct.
Deluxe Streamline Coaches: Bangor to Boston.

PINE TREE
No. 14 via Augusta
Carries M. C. through coaches
B&M-MC Parlor Car 140 Bangor to Boston. D.R.
Restaurant Lounge Car: Bangor to Boston (7 15 AM
to 1 10 PM).
Deluxe Streamline Coaches: Bangor to Boston.

No. 19 via Augusta
B&M-MC Parlor Car 190 Boston to Bangor. D.R.
Restaurant Lounge Car: Boston to Bangor (4 30 PM
to 10 00 PM).
Deluxe Streamline Coaches: Boston to Bangor.

No. 21
Coaches: Boston to Portland.

*Timetable roster of memorable B&M name trains frame a glimpse
of the "Day White Mountains"*

4-8-2 "Oliver Wendell Holmes"

P-2d 3629 and, below, P-3a 3700

These trains kept a fleet of engines busy.

We go out to Yard 3 and find the train. Get the equipment out. Hang out the markers, lighted if necessary. Hook up the riding hose—it's an extension to the train line that we can operate from the rear platform—and open the angle cock. Then we go up to the head end, where the engine has just come from the Big House. We hook him on; the car knocker connects up the air. Ever wonder what the two hoses on passenger cars were for? The big one was the air-brake line and the small one the signal line. They were different sizes so we couldn't cross 'em up. The car knocker connects the jointed steam-heat pipe line, too, and a lighting jumper from the rear of the engine tank to the head car—this because our train is made up of old wooden open-platform coaches without lighting generators.

Now we inform the engineer that we will be handling the air on the back-up move. When the train line is charged up, the engineer sets the brakes and the car knocker walks along back to make sure that they are all on. We go back through the cars making sure that the seats are all turned properly, the toilet doors locked. When the car knocker gets to the rear end he signals the engineer to release brakes. We're ready to go.

Three pulls on the signal line is our signal to the engineer to start backing up. Keep an eye out for the first jack; there it is, indication Yellow. However, we have to watch closely the position of the switch. Anyone who has ever backed a draft in from Yard 3 remembers that there used to be an odd jack which—although Yellow—could lead you into a stub track ending up at the Charles River. You had to see the *iron* to be sure you weren't getting trapped. This time OK, and we see the next jack Green. We clank across the interlocking toward Tower "A." At the drawbridge is a Green jack and, as we come in over the bridge, we signal the engineer again with three pulls. This was a requirement; if we hadn't done so, the engineer was supposed to stop. One more clear jack ahead, and we're lined into a station track.

As we move in along the outer platform, keeping an eye out for baggage trucks in a position to foul us, we start making a brake reduction with the valve on the riding hose. Slow 'em down a bit. Further in, we pinch 'em down some more. Now we've slowed to a walk. When we get to within a car length of the bunter, we open the valve wide and give it to 'em. Stopped well short of the bunter, we jump down and close the angle cock. We remove the riding hose, stow it away in the rear of the last car. Passengers start streaming through the gate toward the train.

We stay by the rear steps, helping aboard any women who come to get on at that car platform. Occasionally we sound off: "Wilmington train! West Medford, Winchester, Woburn and Wilmington!" By now the rest of our train crew is on hand; when leaving time comes, the conductor "rings out," using a push button on the station platform near the head end. We already have a Green jack from Tower "A" way up beyond the platform. We pass motions up from the rear end. When we all say "Go" the conductor gives the engineer a motion and we pull out, bell ringing and cylinder cocks whooshing steam. Our markers show red to the rear, green to the front and side.

Over the drawbridge, past Tower "A," we clatter through the interlockings, bang across Hoosack Tunnel diamond and on by the engine house, then up the High Line with Yard 9 on one side, Yard 8 on the other. Soon we're at Mystic Junction, where we see crews humping cars in the yards on both sides. Winter Hill . . . Somerville Junction . . . and we're away through North Somerville and, soon after, Tufts College. We start to slow down for the stop at Medford Hillside.

It's only a short stop here, just enough for us to unload, help off the few passengers for this stop and swing highballs to get going again for West Medford. Not far to there; we barely have time to announce into each car that we're working "West Medford next" before we're slowing down for that station. Quite a gang gets off here and a couple of minutes get used up. We move again as soon as we can, because there's a fast train out of Boston behind us, and we have to be on the Woburn Loop by the time they get to Winchester. They go main line —first stop, Lowell.

Around Bacon's Curve and through Wedgmere, here we come into Winchester. We have a lot of passengers for here and we get 'em off as soon as possible. Up ahead we see a Bottom Green. As we get moving we swing off the main line into the Woburn Loop. Past Cross Street and Woburn Highlands at a more leisurely pace. Lots of grade crossings along here, each with a gate tender. We grind around the S-curve into Woburn and stop with the engine on a crossing way up ahead.

A sizable number of passengers unload, many of them hurrying home for supper. Steam from the traps under each car drifts up and around. Yes, it's a chilly night. Now highballs, and with clanging bell we pull out along the very crooked branch line. After stops at Central Square and North Woburn we're away for Wilmington, a six-minute run. As we approach North Woburn Junction, we have to go out on the rear platform, where we open the valve on the end of the steam-heat line. Steam shoots out to one side with a roar. We signal the engine with one long blast on the signal line; the fireman turns off the steam-heat valve at the head end. Pressure must be off by the time we get to Wilmington, for we have to break the connection when we head pin up there. Steam shortly stops blowing, by which time we're slowing for Wilmington.

Our job terminates here, so that after the station stop we pull up into the Wildcat, from which we'll back the train off into the coach yard. As we haul up by the engine house we take down the markers and stow them inside. When we're over the yard switch we swing him up, drop off and get the iron to a clear track in the yard. Give him a back-up motion now; the train slowly shoves back into the yard.

Somebody stays on the ground near the fouling point and, when the hind end

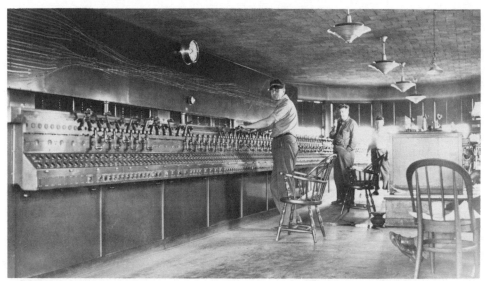

On the job at Tower "A"

swings "Stop," passes the motion to the engineer. Now it's necessary to cut off the air lines and crawl under with a hammer to knock out the wedges on the steam-line connection, and part the connection, hanging each end on a short chain provided. Don't forget to pull out the car-lighting jumper. Pull the head pin and, with a motion, we uncouple and take the engine up to the house-track switch.

Once we line him onto the house track we're all through except to line up and lock all switches, put away the rear-end kit and lock all the car doors. This typical commuter passenger job is finished.

There were many passenger jobs similar to the Wilmington one we just followed. Other such trains put up for the night at Lowell, Stoneham, Bedford, Reading, Rockport, Newburyport, Clinton, Haverhill and Salem. These places all had turntables or wyes, and most of them had engine houses where the Moguls and P-2's simmered away until the morning rush began.

OTHER PASSENGER JOBS

The passenger board was called on not only to cover the through jobs and the locals but other jobs you might not think of as passenger trains. A lot of us won't forget the "Paper Trains" that ran Sunday mornings. We loaded these trains over at "A" House near Lechmere Square, starting around nine or ten Saturday night. About midnight, when the papers were all loaded—and by this time those bundles of Sunday papers were getting mighty heavy—all but the train crew had left for home.

The first train to leave would be No. 1001, consisting of all baggage cars and perhaps one or two coaches. This train left "A" House at 12:00 midnight, backed into the North Station and left there at 12:10. First stop was Dover (N.H.), where they stayed for twenty-nine minutes unloading papers. After that they made Wells Beach, Biddeford, then Portland. Train No. 1003 left "A" House an hour after 1001, left North Station at 1:10 A.M. for stops at every station between Wyoming and Dover to unload papers. Train 1001 was in the public timetable, but this listed no stops between Boston and Portland. No. 1003 appeared only in the employees' timecard.

At 12:55 A.M. No. 3001 left "A" House for the North Station, left there at 1:10 A.M.* and stopped at Wilmington, North Billerica, Lowell, Nashua, Merrimack, Manchester and Concord. This train was not in the public timetable at all.

No. 2001 left the North Station at 2:00 A.M., stopping at Lynn, Salem, Beverly and all further stations to Portsmouth and, apparently, carried no passengers. Train No. 65 left "A" House at 1:30 A.M., did not go to the North Station, but stopped almost everywhere from Waverly to Troy (N.Y.) with instructions, as noted in the employees' timecard, to "run at a speed by non-stop stations which will allow safe delivery of newspaper packages." The public timetable listed this train only between Greenfield and Troy, the only passenger service it provided.

These trains could be back-breakers; those Sunday papers were heavy. The last car on 3001 was "solid Lowell," so that when we pulled into Lowell station the flagman had to beat it back and get his markers off before the Lowell switcher, which was waiting, came to pick this car off.

Other trains covered by the passenger board were:

—The Christmas mail extras, trains of box cars with a coach on the end for the crew. These trains were loaded with mail and Christmas packages at the North Station and sent to the extremes of the system.

—The "Snow Trains," which were very popular beginning in 1931. Must be plenty of people who remember them, and the baggage car set up as a ski shop on Track 2 at the North Station.

—The race trains to Suffolk Downs and back, and the "Rockingham Racers" to Rockingham Park, special trains from Boston in the racing season. They went up with a trainload of hopefuls and came back with a trainload of long faces.

When the race meet was coming to Rockingham we would get the horse extras, not carrying the race fans but carrying the horses. There was a fleet of horse cars resembling baggage cars, only much longer, with wide doors. These cars carried the animals, hay, saddles and whatever other rig went with horse racing, including the handlers. These latter bedded down with a blanket, at the feet of their charges, and rode right along with them.

We usually got these trains from the New Haven at Worcester. With a P-2 on the head end and a coach for a riding car on the hind end, away we'd go for

---

* Yes, same as No. 1003, above.

Awaiting a Green jack from Tower "A"

Rockingham by way of Ayer, Lowell and Lawrence. When the meet was over we'd have the move in reverse. These jobs were called off the passenger spare board at the North Station because the horse cars were designated as passenger equipment.

One time I was called for a horse train, Worcester to Rockingham and return. The whole crew deadheaded to Worcester. When the New Haven connection came in we switched engines and riding cars and took off for Rockingham. When we got to Lawrence there was a trainmaster to meet us. He told us to head pin the engine and pick up a flat car over in Lawrence yard. We were to take this car along with the outfit up the Manchester-Lawrence route to Rockingham, as they needed it up there to use as a loading platform for something. We were to leave the flat car in Lawrence on the way back. We all grumbled as we made this pickup, that is, all except the conductor. He seemed quite happy about it. After we got rid of the trainmaster we found out the reason for the conductor's attitude. Since a flat car is freight equipment and the rate of pay for handling freight equipment was higher than for passenger equipment, we all claimed our time at freight rates for the day, as per union agreement.

Every year in May the circus came to town. Ringling Brothers, Barnum and Bailey Circus had three trains, two of which would come to Boston. The third train went only to places where the show was put on under canvas. Of the other two trains, one was made up of all Pullman cars, the other one of animal cars and flats carrying circus wagons and other equipment. Like the horse trains, we'd get the circus trains from a New Haven connection at Worcester. We'd go out of Boston with two 4100's and two buggies all tied together. At Worcester we usually had to wait for the circus to arrive. Then there'd be all manner of scurrying around before we got straightened away for Boston. There always was a trainmaster on hand, though the circus had its own trainmaster, too. Once under way, the job was no different from any other freight or passenger train move, except that it caused a lot of excitement along the way. When we hauled into Mystic we'd cut off the road engines and the yard switcher grabbed the trains and hauled them down behind the Industrial Building alongside the North Station. There were no particular incidents I especially remember about these jobs unless it was watching the unloading.

Baggage Master

"Baggage Master" was one of the more interesting jobs covered off the passenger board. Three of such jobs on the New Hampshire Division were a car on No. 5 which we covered from Boston to Concord; the car on No. 307 which we worked to White River Junction and back, next day, on No. 320; and the car to White River on No. 325 and, coming back, on No. 332.

We'd have everything in those cars: passengers' checked baggage, mail sacks of parcel post, separate parcel post packages, railroad mail, milk cans, railroad supplies or any odd thing that would fit in through the door. It all had to be written up in reports that we would send on to Boston in Train Mail. In addition to writing it up we had to separate it into piles, so that things could be put off at the proper places.

The first baggage car I ever covered was that on No. 325. I told the crew dispatcher at the North Station that I didn't know the separations, but he told me to go ahead, start loading, and that he would be along with a diagram. He never showed up—and the car was heavy that night. I got mail sacks for towns I'd never heard of, beyond White River, so everything went into one pile. Lowell, Nashua, Manchester and Concord I knew; their stuff was put off right, but the rest went into the pile. At White River they had to haul it all out on baggage trucks, and sort it. I supposed I'd hear complaints about this, but I never did.

No. 325 was due out of Boston at 8:00 P.M. By 7:55 I was loaded so tight that the only room left to stand in was by the doorway. At the last minute they showed up with a casket. This they slid into the last remaining space, and I slid shut the door. From Boston to Lowell I rode sitting on that casket.

Once I had three hampers of snakes belonging to a carnival performer. These were to go from Boston to Concord and in all that distance I didn't take my eyes off them. I was determined, if I saw anything coming out of a hamper, to pull the air and go out the door.

We always dreaded working those cars around the first of the month when Rumford Press in Concord was shipping magazines. A mail sack full of magazines was too heavy to lift off the floor, and we'd have half-a-car full. We called them "stiffs." You'd work your life out handling them.

I used to think the lumberjacks coming down from Canada on No. 332 brought all their axes with them, the trunks in the baggage car were so heavy!

Leaving White River, the car on 320 was usually quite empty. I have sat at one end of those old wooden cars and watched the whole thing twist as we took the curves on down to Concord. But south of Concord we were too busy to watch things twist.

No. 320 picked up a milk car at Enfield, and the baggage masters did the work. We had to crawl under, cut off the air line and knock apart the steam line. Then ride the engine down to get the switch and the derail and back in onto the milk car. Make all the connections and let off the hand brake on the car. Come back onto the train and hook everything up. Got a good workout there.

Also, we picked up cans of milk at many of the way stations north of Concord, most of these going off again at Lowell. Large cans of milk often had insulating jackets on them. Cream traveled in smaller cans.

For some stations where we didn't stop we would have newspapers in bundles or rolls for delivery on the fly. That could be somewhat of an adventure. You'd best not carry papers beyond their destination, news being the perishable commodity it is.

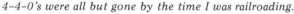

4-4-0's were all but gone by the time I was railroading.

A frequent transient at the Rigby engine terminal

Down East Interlude

ONE MEMBER OF OUR B&M FAMILY WAS THE PORTLAND TERMINAL COMPANY. MANY memories that name brings back! This company ran the Portland area rail service. They maintained Rigby Yard and a big engine terminal there, used not only for the company's own engines but for those of the B&M and Maine Central. PT Co. operated Yard 7 on the north side of Fore River and Yard 5, way around by Back Cove on the north side of Portland itself. They did the switching in South Portland and all the switching down the waterfront along Commercial Street. They also had a local freight run to Cumberland Mills.

Early in the winter of 1948–49 business in Boston fell off so much that the freight board at Mystic was cut—which included me. I couldn't mark up anywhere. Concord and White River boards were full. However, I was told that the Portland Terminal was in need of men on the yard board and, if I wished, I could go there temporarily. So I packed a bag and deadheaded to Portland. The conductor and engineer of the train I went down on were given a message to let me off at Rigby, which they did.

At Rigby I found that the PT had plenty of work, and plenty of snow. I marked up on their board and away I went—eight hours switching, then eight hours rest and right back at it.

There was a little bunkhouse over behind the engine house where transient crews could get a bunk and a locker for twenty-five cents a night. In part of the building a little dining hall provided hot meals. This was very convenient, because there was no place to stay near Rigby. I took up residence in this bunkhouse.

I caught all kinds of jobs, switching both sides of Rigby Yard and in Yard 7. Here we would line up the work for Commercial Street and then go down there to switch the wharves and meat-packing plants, all the time dodging trucks and autos, because the tracks ran right down the middle of the street. Some days we lined up a whole string of empty coal cars and shoved it down Commercial Street to Randall & McAllister's wharf, with the whole crew strung out along the train passing motions. I was usually on the engine end of the job, so that all I had to do was mimic the others. When we'd shoved these cars into the dark recesses of the coal wharf we'd pick up a string of coal loads and back to Yard 7 we'd go.

On jobs to Yard 5 we started from Rigby, went down across the Fore River bridge, swung left and up through Union Station, then out around town to Yard 5. Once we switched there all day in a snowstorm. It was some miserable—half the time I didn't know where I was going, just followed the engine. And it was the same on a day I went down to South Portland on a job handling mostly tank cars, I recollect.

They had a transfer job running back and forth, back and forth, between Yard 7 and Rigby. The night I caught that one, we made about four trips in all. As we pulled out of Rigby for one of these trips, I was standing on the right-hand side talking to the engineer. He said, "Get up here and run her for a while." After explaining what I had to do, he got down and went over to the fireman's side to eat his lunch. We had one of the ex-B&M 600 Class engines, an 0–8–0. These were big engines and I felt as though I had my hands full. I

Diesel haul "down east"

hung out of that cab like Casey Jones, although we were only hauling along slow. I ran that big thing two or three times that night—a thrill I won't forget.

A week or so went by. Then came a night when I went into the yard office to mark up, and they had a message for me from the crew dispatcher at Mystic: to grab a train back to Boston—men needed! Next morning I hooked a ride over to Union Station and from there to Boston rode the cushions. It seems that there had been a big snowstorm around Boston, too, so things were in a mess. One mess led to more, because we started having a series of storms that stretched out over two months. I marked up first out.

SNOW

That winter of 1948–49 there was so much snow that there was no place to plow it all. Everything ran late. Some cars in sidings didn't move for a week, or more. When they could get the yards dug out enough to make up a train, they would run a local which oftentimes "canned"✽ before finishing its schedule. Help was so scarce on the Mystic boards they had to bring shop help down from Billerica, give them a timecard and a switch key and put them out braking.

Now having one of these fellows was not quite the same as having nobody, but almost. None of them were qualified flags and none of them knew the road. This wasn't their fault, of course, but—after wading through hip-deep snow all day, digging out every switch that had to be thrown, and replacing knuckles because engines tried to start cars that were all bogged down—to have one of these machinists along was hardly a joyous thing. They didn't dare step off a moving engine, so you had to stop and let them off, then stop to pick them up—only sometimes when you stopped you didn't start up again. As I said, it wasn't their fault. They were as miserable as the rest of us, and maybe more so because they didn't know what to do.

Plowing snow that winter was quite something. Picture this scene: It's been snowing for two or three hours, and now it's starting to blow as well. You call the crew dispatcher to find out how you stand. He tells you you're six times out. You remark that it looks as though you'll finally get some rest. He tells you to get your rest all right because the storm is supposed to go all night, and you know what that means.

You check your car, get out of your snow clothes and hit the bed early. Sure enough, at 11 P.M. the phone rings. You're called for a snowplow at 3:00 A.M., so that's the end of the rest. You get dressed, eat a hot meal, fill your bag plumb full of lunch and it's out into the storm. First thing, of course, is to dig your car out again.

When you get to Mystic you find the outfit in Yard 9: a plow, a K-8 2–8–0 and a buggy. Instructions are to plow the main line north to Lowell and back, cleaning all passing tracks, Wilmington yard and Swanton Street yard in Win-

---

✽ To can—to reach Federal limit of sixteen hours of continuous duty and, therefore, go off duty. Only a message bearing Superintendent's signature permitted this limit to be exceeded. Limit since reduced.

chester. Nothing has gone out since 10:30 last night and PB-4 is stuck on the Wildcat. It's blown up to a blizzard, and drifting. Things are going to be just dandy.

The conductor goes for the lineup. The section foreman hasn't shown up yet because his car is stuck, so there's time to look the outfit over. B&M had two types of plows, single-track and double-track. The single-tracks were wedge plows that threw snow to both sides, whereas a double-tracker threw it all to the right-hand side of the track. The single-track plows were more likely to stay on the iron because, when you hit into a heavy drift, the force was the same on each side. But the double-track plows tried to bounce to the left whenever they came up against something solid.

Both types had adjustable "wings" which could be extended so as to toss the snow away from the track as far as possible. After all, tomorrow you're going to have to have some place to plow the snow that fell today and, after that, the next day. The wings were extended or retracted either mechanically or pneumatically. They were retracted for close clearances, if not, the results could be spectacular! The plows were also equipped with "flangers"—rail scrapers—that had to be hauled clear at each switch, grade crossing, hand-car takeoff and so forth. Trackside flanger markers were placed in advance of these situations so that the operators on the snowplows could pull the flangers clear of such obstacles as switch points, diamonds or any condition that would wreck the flangers themselves. The flanger markers were boards painted yellow, with two black dots, mounted at a 45° angle on supporting uprights.

Crew in charge of the flangers rode along with the conductor and plow operator in a monitor similar to the monitor on a buggy. They had to be on their toes because, when plowing a lot of snow, it took very little distance for the cab windows of the pusher engine to become so plastered with snow that the engineer couldn't see a thing. There was a rig tied in with the engine whistle, but controlled from the plow monitor, that took place of the usual motions. When the crowd in the monitor wanted to go ahead or back up they whistled the engineer accordingly. If they wanted to stop, they could do so because they had control of the air.

To ride one of those plows was an adventure because, when bucking heavy snow, you heard noises in there that you never knew existed. Nobody except those in the monitor could see anything or really know what was happening. Any others just hovered near the pot-bellied stove. In any case, it was hard to keep your mind off that big K-8 shoving right behind you. If, suddenly, the plow derailed, that thing back there would keep right on coming.

While all the above things may have crossed your mind, the section foreman and other crew are on hand; the wait to get going is over. We push out of the lead at 3:30 A.M. When we get out to Winter Hill there's a Red jack. There we stop. Someone goes to the phone box; what does Mystic Tower have to say?

Mystic replies he can't get the iron. All right, take a look and see what's wrong. What's wrong is that the switch heater has gone out and, naturally, the section gang is somewhere else. The interlocking switch is snowed in, also frozen—it's shovel and sweep until the tower can get the iron. It kills some time.

In due course, we're out and moving. Everything goes smoothly until we get to North Somerville. (Anyone who knows the area will tell you we haven't gone far.) A passing track between North Somerville and Tufts College has to be cleaned out. We drop off a flagman and go plowing up the main line to Tufts, then back down to North Somerville again. Meantime, some of the gang has been cleaning out the switch. Pick up the flag. Shove into the passing track and plow up through that one, now also covered with the snow we plowed off the main line (even though the plow tried to wing it over as far as the wing makes possible).

After digging out the switch at Tufts we get back onto the main line. From here to West Medford is not too bad, but the headlight on the plow is so plastered with snow that no one can see much. When we get to West Medford we find that the highway plows have plowed it up plenty, right across the B&M tracks. We hit it hard. OK, but we have trouble, because the flanger operator doesn't get his flangers up quite soon enough; something underneath goes haywire. We stop at the station, the gang gets under to fix that mess. The flagman goes back yet again. It's 4:45 when we get moving once more.

Around Bacon's Curve and through Wedgemere the going is pretty good. The gang at Winchester has cleaned the crossing, so that things go along all right as the outfit heads up toward Winchester Highlands. Right after the Highlands are the cuts at Montvale, a different story—the K-8 feels it, so does everybody else. We shove on to South Wilmington, where there is a siding we can't head into. It's back in, and plow out. This siding is not a consignee's track. It's up to the B&M—meaning us—to clean it.

Consignees were responsible for plowing their tracks right up to the derail. Sometimes they did a good job. Sometimes they didn't. If a consignee's track looked like a mess, in conditions such as I've described, we might not go in to do switching. However, we might as often take a chance, and—on the way in or out—BUMP, BUMP, BUMP, a car goes on the ground.

Now the fun begins. Try manhandling rerailing frogs in snow up to your midriff. Eventually you'll get them in position—and the car back on the rails—but, after three or four times a day, you tend to feel a mite jaded, not to say cold. Howsomever, so far so good. Just think, it could have been the plow off the tracks or—a *real* joy—the engine!

We're at South Wilmington, snow pelting down. We have to plow out the siding, or enough of it to *say* we did. We consider that the engine is heavier than the buggy, so that it makes good sense to cut the buggy off on the main line and back in on the siding, hauling the plow. We plow it out, as much as we can.

Pick up the buggy and go along. We're all right until we get to Wilmington, and there the signal is ALL RED.

Conductor calls Winchester. The message is that the trainmaster wants us to go into Wilmington and clean out the yard enough so that passenger trains can be made up, then plow up the Wildcat as far as PB-4 so that someone can do something about getting them going. They will be on short time soon. The section gang at Wilmington has been working on the switches; now most of them can be thrown. We nose up through the passing track and, somewhere on the curve, it happens—the plow goes on the ground!

Things liven up, what else? Everyone is running around looking for blocking and jacks. The section crew breaks out shovelers they didn't know they had. Our engine needs water. A trainmaster appears out of nowhere; at a time like this you *need* him. This kind of situation can go on and on. In fact, we'll probably can in Lowell. This is the way it went during that winter of 1948–49.

On the locals that actually ran life was no easier. I went out on the Bedford local one day. We ran into considerable drifting that had piled up after the plow had gone through. We pushed on to a point between Billerica and Bennett Hall, and stuck. We had a Mogul and five cars, one of which was a milk car. The drifts were so bad that the only way we could move was to take one car at a time to Bennett Hall—five trips altogether—and bang in the middle of these moves we had to go down to Billerica Shop to take water. That night we canned in Lowell.

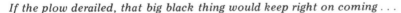

If the plow derailed, that big black thing would keep right on coming . . .

. . . all the wrecked cars over to one side.

12   "Derailments"

WRECKS ARE A SUBJECT THAT RAILROADS DON'T LIKE TO HAVE BROUGHT UP; THEY reflect on the railroad's operating and maintenance procedures. But wrecks happen—on the B&M we called them "derailments"— and I'd like to tell about two that I well remember. Actually, during my years on the B&M we had very few wrecks, and no loss of life that I ever heard of. I can recall only one incident that involved a passenger train.

That one passenger incident happened at Canaan, N.H. This unfortunate happening, I feel, as did many others, was the result of habit. A person does something day after day; it becomes a habit. Then, when conditions change, the habit does not and it causes trouble.

For years, northbound train No. 307 would meet southbound No. 332 at Canaan. This meet was shown in the employees' timecard. Because 307 and 332 were both First Class trains, one had to be ruled superior to the other. The rule is that inward trains are superior to outward trains: this made 332 superior to 307 by direction. Therefore, 332, the superior train, held the main line at Canaan; 307 took the siding.

Normally, No. 332 would arrive at Canaan first, since they had to come only a short way from White River, while No. 307 had to come all the way from Boston.

Furthermore, 307 quite often ran late. What usually happened was that the baggage master of 332 would walk up to the passing track switch and have it open for 307, thereby saving 307 some time and expediting the meet.

As I recollect, it was in August, 1949, when, with No. 307 running heavy and late, the dispatcher issued an order to both trains, to the effect that on this particular day No. 332 was to take the siding. This order made 307 superior *by right* and allowed them to pull directly through on the main line. The trap was set.

As usual, No. 332 arrived first and pulled in on the passing track as per order. But the baggage master, apparently from force of habit, walked up to the switch and, when he heard 307 coming around a curve beyond an overhead bridge, he opened the switch. This lined 307 head-on into 332.

All kinds of whistle blowing by the engine crew of No. 332 failed to show the baggage master that he had done wrong. No. 307 popped under the bridge, saw the open switch too late and went into 332 at about thirty miles an hour.

Though a number of people were hurt, there were no fatalities, a result that was most likely due to the presence of a wooden milk car directly behind 307's diesel. This old wooden car collapsed. It acted like a big spring, absorbing the shock that otherwise would have been transmitted right back to the passenger cars. The diesels were completely wrecked. I believe they were No. 3807 and the 4225.

Two days later I was called to cover the baggage master's job on No. 307, in place of the regular man who had been pretty well shaken up in the wreck. No orders were issued. We were to meet 332 in the normal manner, in other words, we were to take the siding. As we pulled around under the bridge at Canaan I was preparing to unload and go up to get the switch. No. 332 was already there on the main line and the baggage master of 332, also a spare man, had the switch open for us.

The other wreck I recall took place at what was called "AR" Tower between Kennebunk and Biddeford. This one was a high-wheel freight that burned off a journal, dragging it along for half a mile until it hit the crossovers at "AR," where everything piled sky high.

I was called early next morning for a work train to go from Boston to Billerica Shop, where they loaded all kinds of track material into our open gondolas. This consisted of spikes, tie plates, connector bars and what not. Then we went up to Lowell, turned on the New Haven wye and moved east over the Lowell Junction Branch to Lowell Junction and then north up the Portland Division.

We had left Boston early in the morning so arrived at Dover, N.H., before noon, where we were instructed to stop at every rail stand beyond North Berwick and pick up all spare rails. We were also supposed to pick up every tie pile as well. We were to work up the outward main to the scene of the wreck. They had the inward main open around the pile up and were running all trains over it in a single-iron operation. Because we were swinging the crane on our outfit, we had to do some real flagging.

It was wintertime, although there was no snow. It was mighty cold. Nobody had a chance to eat. I had a couple of sandwiches with me, but that was all. No chance to get warm or get any coffee. By late in the afternoon we had worked our way up as close as we could go to the wreck. They had piled all the wrecked cars over to one side. The smashed wooden ones were being burned up. It was quite a mess!

Of course, we were getting on short time and could not possibly reach Boston. It was arranged to have a train crew come down from Rigby to relieve us. The arrangement included taking us from the scene of the wreck by automobile over the road to Biddeford, there to get a passenger train to Boston. This same train was to bring down the relief crew from Rigby, letting them off at Biddeford. But someone wasn't thinking straight. To start with, our engine crew couldn't leave the engine unattended until a relief crew came on the scene. And some other things weren't working out either, as follows.

Half frozen, we all went over to the wrecker's diner to get some coffee but the cook refused us, saying that his supplies were for the wrecker's crew. The Superintendent of the Portland Division, Charles Came, was on hand, and he got wind of what was going on. There was an operator on duty at the scene of the wreck. Came had him send a message to Biddeford to have the passenger train stop at the wreck to exchange crews. This would save us an hour or so of time. Then he got ahold of the wrecker's cook and told him:

"Feed these men."

To us he said, "Take your time, boys. We'll stop that train right here to pick you up. Just be ready when it arrives."

That's the kind of man Charley Came was.

We ate—ham and eggs, home fries, toast, pie—and washed it down with quarts of coffee. When the passenger train came we climbed on and slept all the way to Boston.

Sights and sounds we won't experience again . . .

13   Vanishing Markers

WELL, THESE HAVE BEEN SOME OF MY MEMORIES OF RAILROADING AND WHAT IT was like to have been a brakeman on the Boston & Maine twenty to twenty-five years ago. I could go on—about the weed burners and sprayers, how atrocious the spray smelled and how many of us, including me, were allergic to it. Or the time we stopped to put a hobo off BU-1, only to discover we'd been fooled by a vent pipe on a milk car. Or B&M's own streamliner, the 6000, train of many names: *Flying Yankee, The Minuteman* and so forth.

Almost all I've talked about has changed, or faded away. Trains run, diesels haul and buggies still roll on the hind end, but the steam engines, if not scrapped, are museum pieces, or tourist attractions and—in 1976—the marker lights, which were a fixture on trains for a hundred years, have followed the steamers around the bend into oblivion. They use battery-powered, flashing red gadgets now. These show only red to the rear and, oftentimes, they are missing entirely. Other sights and sounds we won't experience again are—

—The two order boards at Wakefield Junction.

111

—The old center-monitor buggies on the Hillbilly.

—The Wilmington local pounding up over the Yard 9 hump at Mystic on its way out each morning.

—Twenty-three tracks full of evening commuter trains at the North Station, each headed by a steam engine.

—The baggage trucks hauled by little tractors at the North Station.

—The snow melters made from old engine tanks and pushed by one of the 4000 Class engines.

—Open platform passenger coaches.

—PB-4 doubling over at Dover with the brakemen decorating the tops and passing motions to the head end.

—Light engines to Billerica Shop, a smoky red lantern hanging on the rear of the tank.

—The wooden water tank by the Wilmington engine house, the "bear trap" switch at the connection of the New Haven tracks and the Lowell wye, the shanty we called the "oil house" behind the Railway Express Agency at the North Station.

And so forth. When changes were made, they always did it in the name of Progress. Now it has not been my intention to take sides, or to argue that the inefficiencies of conventional, old-time railroading were good things, but only to set down what is in my memory and remains part of my life. However, having known the old ways and seen some Progress, so called, too, I sometimes wonder where we're really at. Are things so much better today than yesterday? By way of comparison, let's imagine the following: It's five o'clock and time to go home from work—

By Auto

Rush out to the car. Sooner we get out there the sooner we'll get ahead of the crazy gang coming out after us. Here's the car. Look at that scratch on the fender. What clown did that? Hope the old bucket holds together at least until it's paid for. Get in. Boy, it's hot in here! Get started up. Watch out for that jerk. What's he backing up here for? Blow the horn. Well, we're finally out of the lot. Go like mad and make that light. Just barely. Now for the expressway. Look at 'em go! Hot pavement. Come on, what do you think this is, a funeral? Duck around this

By Train

Walk down to the station. Time enough. Train leaves at 5:25. Stop in the station to pick up a paper. Train is ready. Go out through the gate. Trainman standing there. "Hi, Joe. Keeping you busy?" Here's our coach. Climb up. Boy, air-conditioning feels good. Some guys getting set for a card game. "Playing tonight, Ernie?" "No, I think I'll just read the paper." Five twenty-five; we're on our way. Ticket in the hat band. Car clacking over the interlocking. Conductor comes by picking up tickets. Stops a minute to ask how the ball game came out. A few station guy. A few miles of this. Look at that truck belch black exhaust. Can't breathe that much longer, so we'll go around. Wow, that was a close one! Now what? A big stoppage. Creep along, bumper to bumper. Car heating up. Never going to get home at this rate. Look at that now, a real smash. Look at that baby on its side! Wonder if anyone hurt? Now, maybe, we can get someplace. Watch out for the cops. Home at last, late as usual. Hot and tired. Supper getting cold. "What do you mean, where was I?" Supper spoiled. Well, I'm not hungry any more . . .

stops. Some of the gang leaves. Finally our station. Get up and stretch. "See you fellows tomorrow. Going to the clambake Saturday, Henry?" Get off and head down the platform as the flagman waves a highball. Train pulls out as we cut across by the gate tender's shanty. "Evening, Mike. How's the missus?" "Fine, Ernie. Take it easy." Walk up the street as the church clock strikes six, right on time. Wonder what's for supper? The whistle of the P-2 drifts back from up the line . . .

Time was when the Boston & Maine made a hit with an advertising campaign that won a prize and made people feel that it was a good thing to have a railroad around. The ads started off, "That's a H—l of a Way to Run a Railroad!" and described some of the hang-ups we had that delayed trains and drew complaints from irascible passengers, but at the same time let people in on what it takes to keep the trains running. Now, just as this book is being made up for the printer, I see that the B&M wants to steer clear of the new Conrail setup that's supposed to bail out the broke Northeastern railroads. If B&M "goes it alone," will they make a go of it?

Wonder if I could get a job braking again, with only my memories to qualify me, memories of the P-2's and K-8's, BU-3 and BP-5, of Mystic and Rigby and White River—and those vanishing markers. . . .

APPENDIX A   Glossary of B&M Terms

ALL BLACK.   A term signifying no hot boxes in sight after having looked over a moving freight train from either end.

ANGLE COCK.   A lever operated valve on each end of a car's brake pipe (train pipe) to which is attached the air hoses. Each piece of rolling stock has an angle cock on each end.

BARN CAR.   A car attached to a maintenance-of-way crane, half of which is enclosed for use of the crane operator, other half is open with tool bins.

BEAR TRAP.   A switch at the west end of the New Haven wye at Lowell which had a queer link contraption which allowed the use of both B&M and New Haven switch locks.

BUGGY.   Caboose.

CAN.   To reach Federal limit of sixteen hours of continuous duty and therefore to go off duty. Only with a message bearing Superintendent's signature could limit be exceeded. Under Public Law 91-169, H.R. 8449, effective Dec. 26, 1970, the 16-hour "Hog Law" was dropped to 14, with further drops mandatory in 1972.

CAR KNOCKER.   Car inspector.

CLOWN'S TENT.   Caboose.

CROSS THE ROAD.   To cross over from one main line to another as from inward main to outward main.

CROSSOVER.   Switches and track used to Cross the Road.

CROSSING.   Highway grade crossing.

DIAMOND CROSSING.   One track crossing another at grade without switches but with frogs only as at Hoosack Tunnel Diamond at Boston and as at White River or Bellows Falls.

DECORATE.   To get on top of box cars in order to pass motions. No longer allowed.

DERAIL.   A heavy iron casting positioned by a stand similar to a switch stand and so shaped that when properly set on top of a rail it will cause the derailment of any car that passes over it. Every consignee's side track must have one to prevent cars from running out to foul the main line.

DOUBLE IRON.   Double track.

DRAFT.   A string of passenger cars not open for passengers and usually a back-up move as between Yard 3 and North Station.

DYNAMIC BRAKE. A braking system on a diesel locomotive which is actuated by the engine's rolling momentum turning the traction motors as generators. Current so generated is dissipated in resistor grids in the roof of the engine.

GET THE IRON. Throw a switch for movement of trains.

GRAB A HANDLE. Climb onto a ladder or grab irons of a car to ride the move. Usually car in motion.

HAND BOMBER. Hand-fired steam engine.

HANDLE THE AIR. To be in charge of the air brake valve. Usually a man in charge of the actual movement of a train handles the air.

HEAD PIN. Knuckle or coupler on rear of the engine. To head pin the engine is to cut the engine off of the train.

HIGHBALL. An OK motion either with a lamp or with the hand. Covers a multitude of situations but means "Everything all right. Go along."

HIGH LINE. That section of New Hampshire Division between the Boston engine terminal and Mystic hump which runs on a high embankment.

HIGH GREEN. Green over two reds on a home signal.

HIGH-WHEEL. A term meaning a through freight. BM-1, MP-2, B-11, all high-wheel jobs.

HITCH. To make a coupling between cars.

HOOK HER UP. To shorten the cutoff of steam on a steam engine by adjusting the valve gear with the reverse lever. Allows engine to run without using as much steam.

HOT RAIL. A shouted alarm or warning to men on or near a track that a train is approaching.

IRON. Track or rails.

JACK. A dwarf signal.

JOKER. The independent or engine brake.

MONITOR. Cupola of caboose.

MOTION. A signal with hand or lamp which calls for movement of a train.

ON THE B. Diesel locomotive operating on the dynamic brake.

PIN. Coupling pin. To "get the pin" is to unlock knuckles with lever provided.

PINCH 'EM DOWN. Apply brakes to a train to slow down.

PULL THE AIR. To apply air brakes from back on the train by opening a train line air valve.

RIDING CAR. A passenger car coupled onto the rear of a train of freight cars or baggage cars for the crew to ride in instead of a buggy.

SCOOP. Coal shovel on a steam engine.

SHORT TIME. To reach fourteen hours of continuous duty at which time the conductor should notify the dispatcher that they have only two hours until they "can" (which see).

SINGLE IRON.   Single track.

STAGGER BLOCK.   A two-light block signal with lights so arranged as to be staggered instead of in a vertical array. It is the approach to a home signal. See section on signals.

STRAIGHT IRON.   Straight track.

STRAIGHTEN THE IRON.   To throw a switch to allow a main line move as opposed to a turn-out move.

STRIPPER.   A manila form which is lined and used to write a switch list on.

SWING HIM UP.   To give the engineer a stop motion.

THREE-ARM POLE.   A home signal either with three semaphore arms or three color light signals.

TURN ON A WHEEL.   To pull into a terminal and leave on return trip without taking rest.

UNLOAD.   To get off of a train.

Ⓑ Roster of B&M Steam Engines

Numbers	Class	Driver Diam.	Pressure	Cyl. Diam.	Weight	Builder	Date
			0–6–0 (SWITCHER)				
200–309	G-10	52	160	19x24	127,800	Manchester	1903 '10
400–429	G-11a	52	200	19x26	147,700	"	1911 '13
430–452	G-11b	52	185	20x26	150,000	Brooks	1916
			0–8–0 (SWITCHER)				
610–631	H-2a	52	175	25x28	221,000	Alco	1922
640–647	H-3a	52	250	23x28	244,800	Baldwin	1928
648–649	H-3a	52	250	23x28	244,800	" °	1928
650–654	H-3b	52	250	23x28	243,200	"	1929
			4–4–0 (AMERICAN)				
1001–1025	A-41	69	190	18x24	115,000	Manchester	1900 '11
			2–6–0 (MOGUL)				
1393–1498	B-15	63	200	19x26	142,400	Manchester	1903 '10

° Had tender booster

Numbers	Class	Driver Diam.	Pressure	Cyl. Diam.	Weight	Builder	Date
			2–8–0 (Consolidation)				
2386–2422	K-7	61	200	20x30	170,000	Alco	1905 '10
2641–2709	K-8b	61	200	24x30	219,400	Baldwin	1913
2711–2734	K-8c	61	200	24x30	219,400	Brooks	1916
			2–10–2 (Santa Fe)				
3004–3014	S-1a	61	190	29x32	377,800	Alco	1920
3021–3027	S-1b	61	190	29x32	372,100	"	1923
2900–2909	S-1c	61	190	29x32	369,200	"	1920
			4–4–2 (Atlantic)				
3205–3244	J-1	79	200	19x28	159,600	Alco	1902 '09
			4–6–2 (Pacific)				
3600–3606	P-1	73	200	22x28	236,700	Alco	1910
3620–3659	P-2d	73	200	22x28	247,700	"	1911
3660–3679	P-2b	73	200	22x28	247,700	"	1913
3680–3689	P-2c	73	200	22x28	244,800	"	1913
3700–3709	P-3a	73	200	24x28	263,800	"	1923
3710–3714	P-4a	73	260	23x28	339,200	Lima	1934
3715–3719	P-4b	73	260	23x28	339,800	"	1937
3696–3699	P-5a	62	210	25x28	300,500	Brooks	1924
			2–8–4 (Berkshire)				
4007–4017	T-1a	63	240	28x30	393,000	Lima	1928
4020–4024	T-1b	63	240	28x30	403,000	"	1929
			4–8–2 (Mountain)				
4100–4104	R-1a	66	240	28x31	416,100	Baldwin	1935
4105–4109	R-1b	66	240	28x31	416,100	"	1937
4110–4112	R-1c	66	240	28x31	414,960	"	1939
4113–4117	R-1d	66	240	28x31	415,200	"	1941

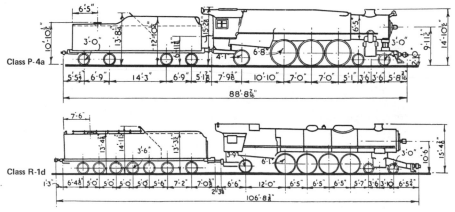

Ⓒ Rush Hour Trains from North Station
Boston Terminal Yards

Train No.	Time	Destination
3329	4.45	Wilmington
3109	4.52	Clinton
147	4.55	Portland
241	4.55	Portsmouth
149	4.58	Reading
2535	4.58	Rockport
2219	5.00	Marblehead
1311	5.01	Danvers *via* Wakefield Jct.
2537	5.03	Rockport
245	5.05	Lynn
3331	5.05	Woburn
2109	5.12	Lynn *via* Saugus Br.
151	5.14	Dover
315	5.14	Nashua
515	5.14	Fitchburg
153	5.16	Reading
5509	5.16	Fitchburg
155	5.17	Reading
3333	5.17	Wilmington
3111	5.17	Clinton *via* Central Mass. Div.
2415	5.19	Danvers *via* Salem
3215	5.20	Bedford *via* Lexington Br.
2221	5.22	Marblehead
517	5.22	So. Acton
1315	5.28	Topsfield *via* Wakefield Jct.
3413	5.30	Stoneham
157	5.32	Lawrence
2539	5.33	Rockport
159	5.35	Reading
520	5.35	So. Acton
247	5.36	Portsmouth
1317	5.38	Wakefield Center
2113	5.38	Lynn *via* Saugus Br.
319	5.40	Lowell
3217	5.43	Bedford *via* Lexington Br.
3335	5.50	Wilmington
3117	5.50	Clinton *via* Central Mass. Div.
2223	5.54	Marblehead
161	5.55	Haverhill
3417	6.00	Stoneham
251	6.01	Portsmouth
163	6.05	Reading
61	6.05	Greenfield
3337	6.15	Wilmington
165	6.20	Reading
3223	6.24	Bedford
2541	6.25	Rockport
323	6.35	Lowell

D Schematic Diagram, N.H. Division

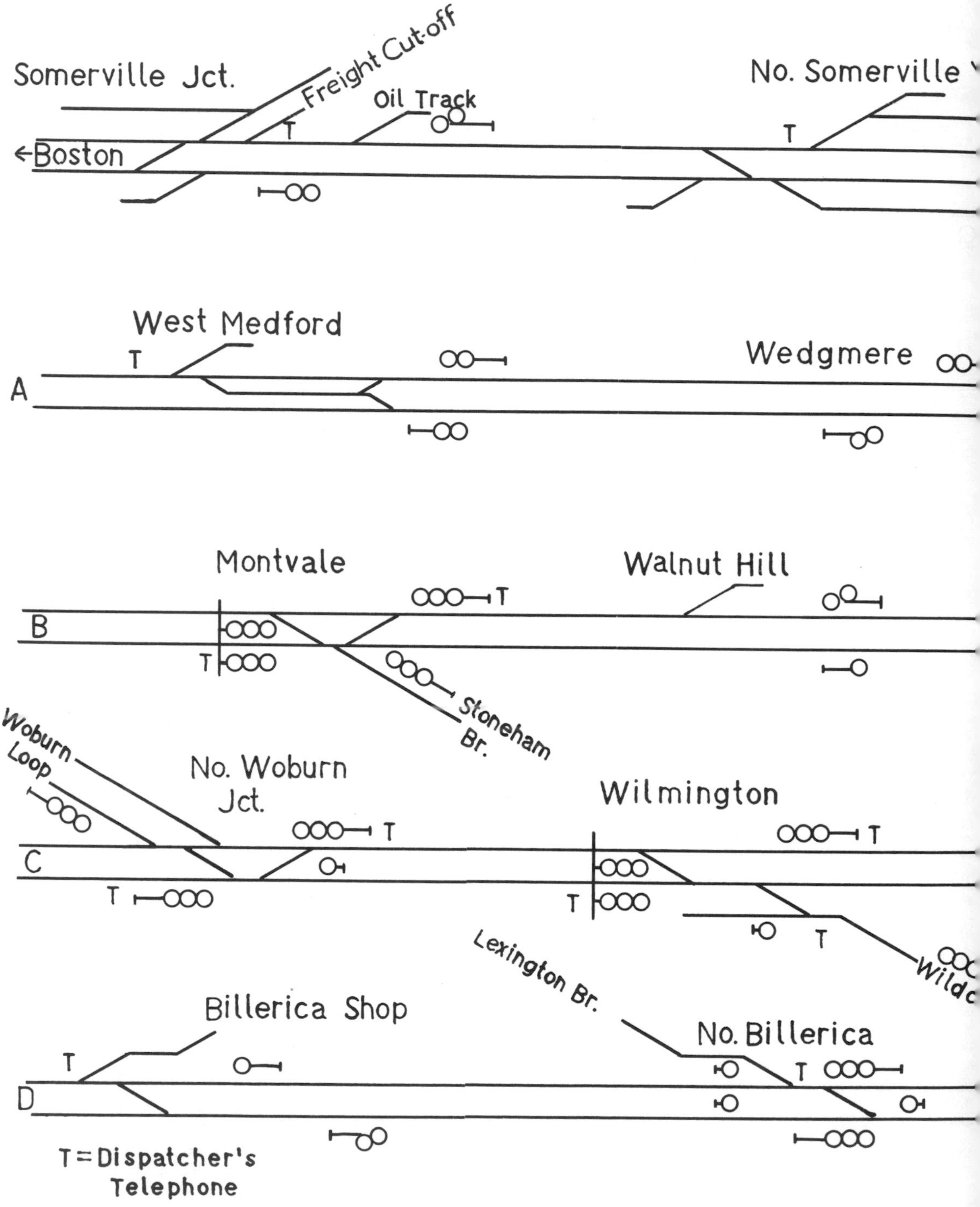

Somerville Jct.

Freight Cut-off

Oil Track

No. Somerville

T

←Boston

West Medford

T

Wedgmere

A

Montvale

Walnut Hill

T

B

T

Stoneham Br.

Woburn Loop

No. Woburn Jct.

Wilmington

T

C

T

T

Wildc

Lexington Br.

Billerica Shop

No. Billerica

T

T

D

T = Dispatcher's Telephone

Drawn by Ralph E. Fisher

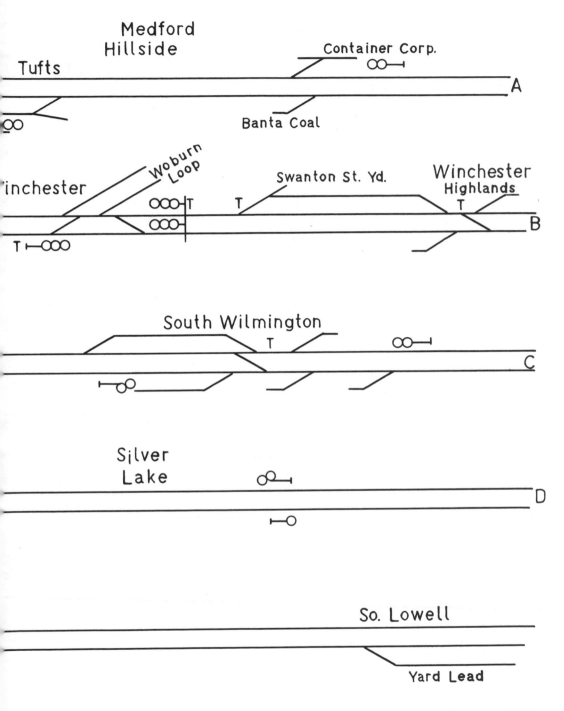

See following pages for B&M diagram ZN-4, North Billerica to Bleachery. See pages 88-89 for Lowell diagram.

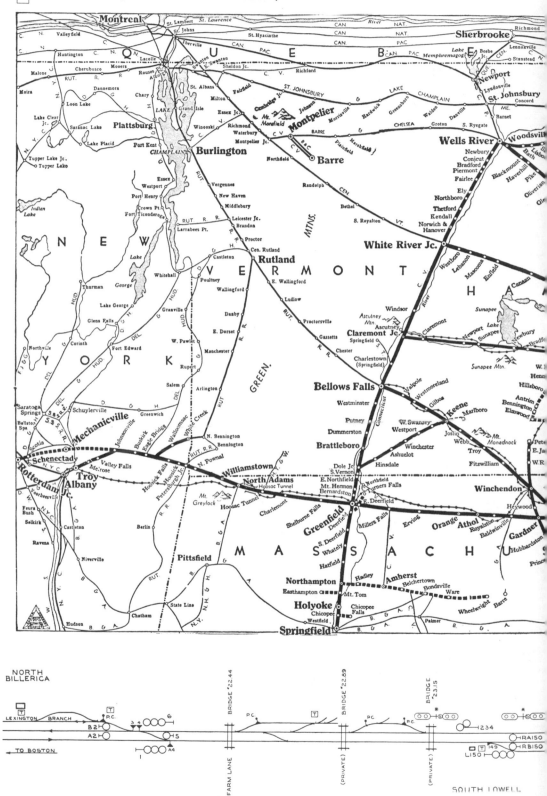

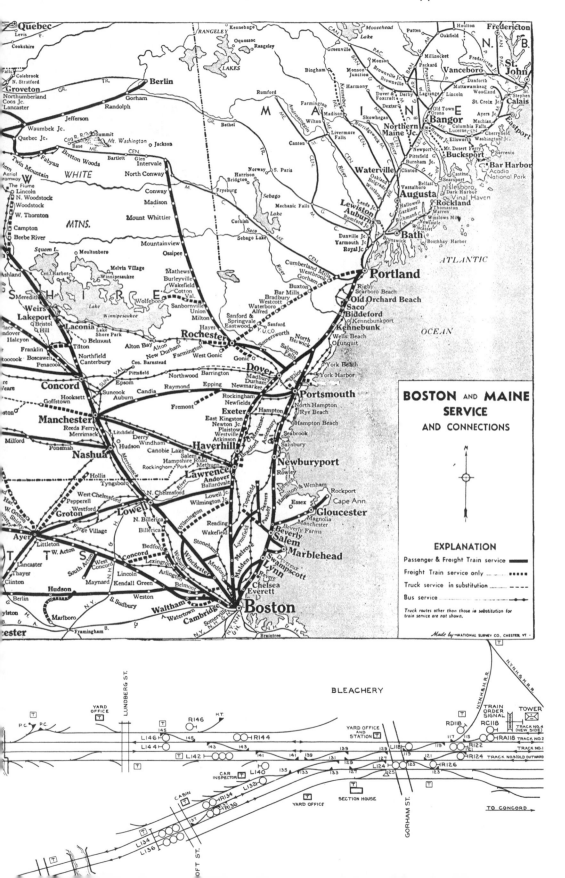

System Map from Employees' Timetable, April 1963

During the years between 1947, the date of issue of the Employee's Timetable from which a facsimile page appears in the chapter "Night Freight," and the 1963 Employee's Timetable featuring the map reproduced here, the number of pages listing First Class trains shrank from seventy-one to twenty-two, dramatic evidence of the curtailment of passenger service—a lot of vanished markers! The photo above, of the CTC panel at Gardner, Mass., with Dispatcher Dugas on duty, is by Donald S. Robinson.

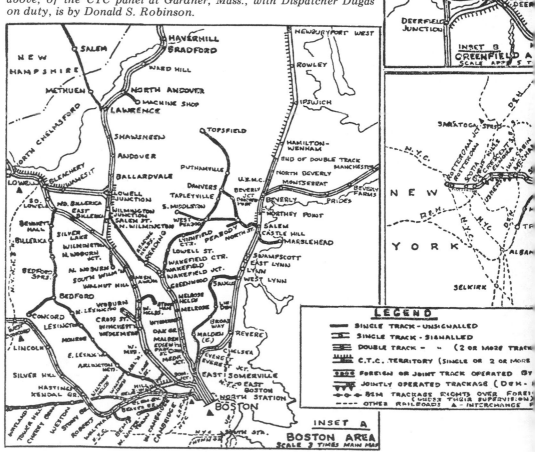

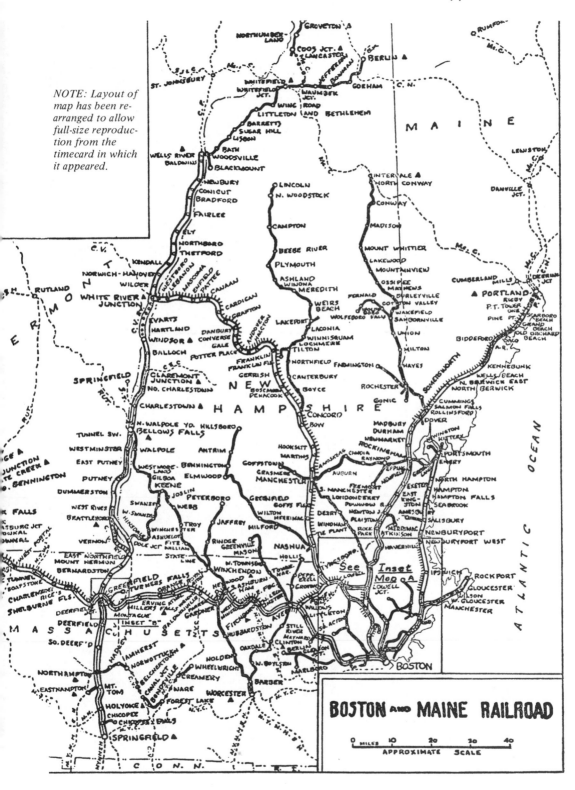

NOTE: Layout of map has been re-arranged to allow full-size reproduction from the timecard in which it appeared.

BOSTON ᴀɴᴅ MAINE RAILROAD

0   MILES 10   20   30   40
APPROXIMATE   SCALE

INDEX